S0-FES-035

mid-1997, Federal Express, the world's largest express transportation company, opened a completely automated hub that includes seven buildings, aircraft ramp areas and parking for delivery trucks. Galaxy Aerospace, manufacturer of the Astra CPX and Galaxy corporate jets, recently moved into a state-of-the-art hangar and headquarters at Alliance.

To make the Alliance transportation system complete, the Burlington Northern Santa Fe Railroad opened a 735-acre, $115 million intermodal yard in April of 1994. This versatile shipping method uses special containers that are loaded onto other trucks, railcars or steamships. Shippers, therefore, can move products from their place of origin to their destination without ever having to unload goods or change receptacles. The intermodal system gives companies the freedom to move products long distances at less cost.

With its sophisticated air, rail and highway access at one central location, Alliance truly has become an "inland port" that has caught the attention of numerous international companies. Firms such as Nokia (Finland), Nolato (Sweden), Perlos (Finland), Valeo (France) and Recaro (Germany) also benefit from one of the largest foreign trade zones in the United States, which allows them to import and export products and defer U.S. tariffs.

To assist companies in meeting their individual corporate requirements, the 9,600-acre Alliance development is subdivided into distinct geographic sectors. The Alliance Center surrounding the airport, for example, caters to aviation-related companies such as American Airlines and Galaxy Aerospace. Westport at Alliance on the western edge houses the BNSF intermodal and auto loading facility. Alliance Commerce Center, located north of the airport, is a business park geared toward small and medium-sized manufacturing, high-tech, research-and-development, office, and distribution firms. The Alliance Advanced Technology Center is designed to create a new advanced-technology corridor in the area, with Intel as a the anchor tenant. Alliance Gateway offers space for large-scale distributors, manufacturers, and office users such as Ameritrade, AT&T, Randalls, Nokia, Zenith and Nestlé. Alliance Crossing provides 150 acres of space for retail stores, restaurants and service-oriented establishments.

Most recently, Texas Christian University has opened an educational center at Alliance to offer custom-tailored programs designed to meet the needs of the companies anchored there, along with those of the residents of surrounding communities. Located in 16,000 square feet of space in Heritage Commons, TCUglobalcenter at Alliance features a 72-person, state-of-the-art tiered classroom; two 30-person classrooms; two large conference rooms; "teaming areas," flexible meeting/classroom spaces that can be configured to suit the individual needs of the group; and a 2,000-square-foot reception area and marketing center.

In the near future, Hillwood intends to develop the Circle T Ranch, both as a commercial and residential community. During the past year, Hillwood completed land sales there to Fidelity Investments for a 314-acre regional corporate campus and 128 acres to General Growth Properties for a 1.6 million-square-foot super regional shopping center. To accommodate the rapid influx of employees, hundreds of executive-style and upscale homes will be built amid the beauty of rolling hills and thick forests. The 10-year-old Alliance area truly has reason to celebrate, because it has something to offer everyone.

ALLIANCE

Opportunity for Today, Vision for Tomorrow

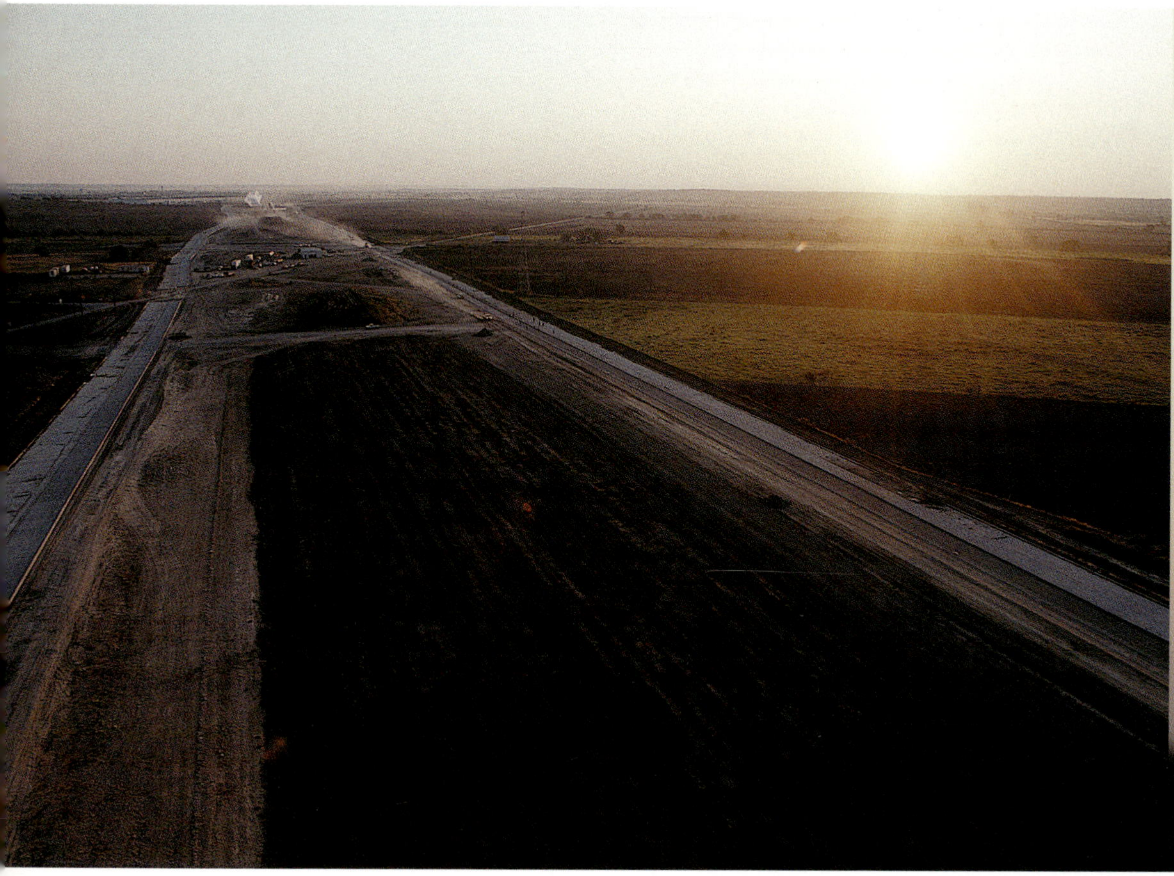
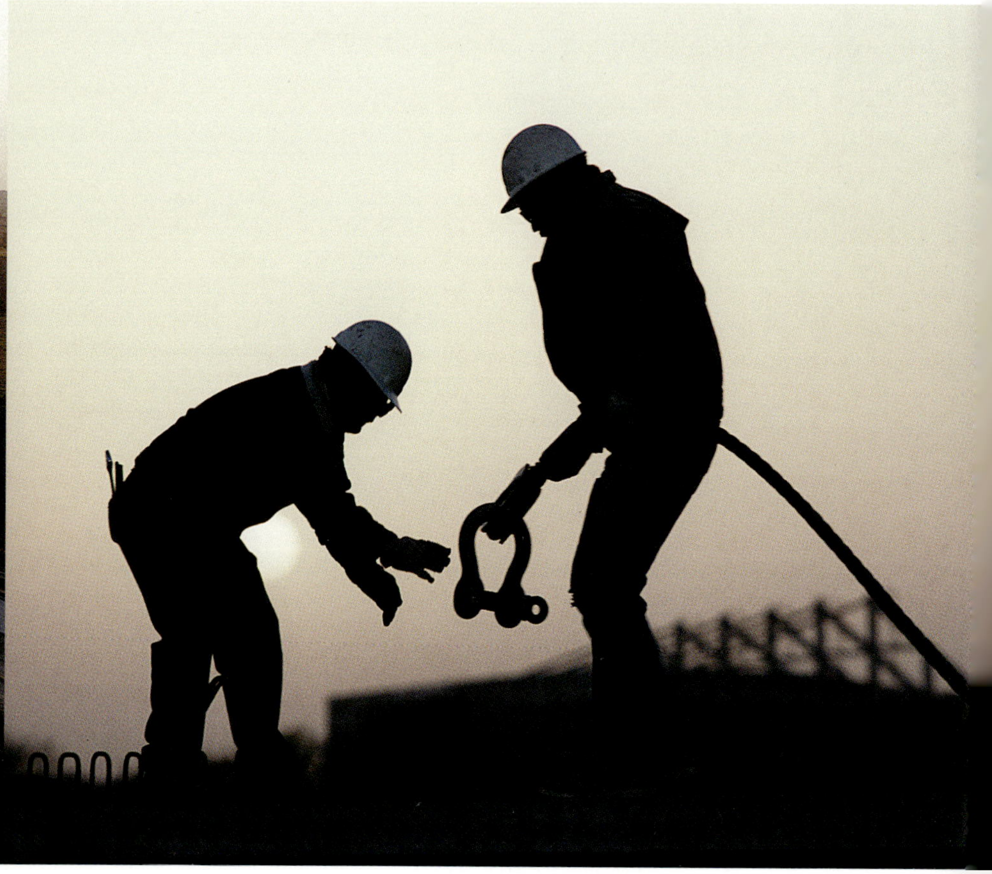

Alliance
A Decade of Success
A New Century of Opportunity

by Mark E. Hanshaw

Photography by Jim Winn

Contributing photographers:
Jeffrey Buehner, Debra Hale, Richard Dalton

MAGNOLIA MEDIA GROUP • FORT WORTH, TEXAS

Copyright © 1999 by Hillwood Development Corporation. All rights reserved. No part of this book may be reproduced or transmitted in any form or by any means, electronic or mechanical, including photocopying, recording or by any information storage and retrieval system without the written permission of the publisher, except where permitted by law.

Published by
Magnolia Media Group
3451 Boston Avenue
Fort Worth, Texas 76116
817-560-6100

Jacket and book design by David Sims

Printed in the United States of America

10 9 8 7 6 5 4 3 2 1

ISBN 0-9653970-3-3

Dedication

This book is dedicated to the people, corporations, governments and employees who played a role in turning the Alliance vision into reality.

VI   ALLIANCE

Allia

Table of Contents

Foreword by Ross Perot Jr IX
Introduction XI

TESTIMONIALS
American Airlines XIII
Burlington Northern Santa Fe Corporation XIV
Nokia XV

CHAPTER ONE
The Vision 1

CHAPTER TWO
Breaking Ground 16

CHAPTER THREE
The Vision Takes Shape 26

CHAPTER FOUR
A Unique Community 42

CHAPTER FIVE
A Vision of the Future 52

A Decade of Success 60
A Decade of Progress 69
Corporate Residents 82

VIII ALLIANCE

Foreword

Alliance, which stands as the only facility of its type in the world, is a great compliment to the people, and to the public and private visionaries who partnered to make the development the great success it is today.

In just 10 years, the development has attracted more than 80 companies, many of them from the Fortune 500. These firms have invested close to $4 billion, created 14,000 full-time jobs and paid more than $59 million in property taxes. The Alliance project is one of the great public-private partnerships in the country, with a 27-to-1 ratio of private investment ($3.8 billion) to public investment ($139 million).

In 1989, we flew prospective customers and civic leaders over vacant fields, talking about a vision of the world's first industrial airport. *Alliance - A Decade of Success, A New Century of Opportunity*, provides in pictures and words how that vision became a reality.

Now the tour has expanded as we fly over the Circle T Ranch, the 2,500-acre development in Westlake, Texas, and Heritage, the 2,500-acre development in north Fort Worth. With these projects in the initial stages of development and the available land at Alliance still only 20 percent developed, we now tell the story of a lifestyle: A master-planned area, straddling Tarrant and Denton counties, providing the latest in technology to allow people to live in a truly wired community. A place hosting some of the best schools in the country and some of the best companies in the world.

None of this would be possible without the tremendous success of Alliance, which has become one of the biggest economic engines in North Texas. The legacy of Alliance will come not only in its future growth, but also in taking much of what was learned at Alliance and incorporating that into some of Hillwood's other projects locally and around the world.

Today, Hillwood is in the initial stages of developing Victory in downtown Dallas. Victory is a 65-acre development that includes American Airlines Center, the new home of the Dallas Mavericks and the Dallas Stars. One of the largest master-planned urban developments in the country today, Victory will bring a new vitality to the city.

Through our newly formed Hillwood Strategic Services division, we take the Alliance story to projects around the world, providing advisory and development services. Many of these services are provided to government agencies and economic development entities that want to replicate Alliance.

As you read about the past decade, dream with us as we continue to build upon the success of Alliance and turn new visions into realities.

ROSS PEROT JR.

Introduction

On July 3, 1999, Alliance kicked off its 10th anniversary celebration with a colorful fireworks show that brightened the evening skies and dazzled visitors. This pyrotechnic presentation, however, could never match the economic "fireworks" that have marked the explosive growth of this master-planned industrial community over the last 10 years. Approximately 2,000 of the 9,600 acres of Alliance have been either leased or sold to more than 80 companies housed in the development. These firms, which include 22 of the Fortune 500, have invested more than $3.8 billion to build more than 14.2 million square feet of space and create 14,000 full-time jobs.

A few years before Alliance broke ground, however, it was difficult to believe that 9,600 acres of prairie land would soon be transformed into a bustling manufacturing and distribution center. Ross Perot Jr., a visionary businessman and former Air Force Reserve pilot, had purchased these huge parcels of land north of Fort Worth only as a real estate investment. Yet, with the encouragement of the Federal Aviation Administration (FAA) and Fort Worth city leaders, Perot set out to build the world's first industrial airport.

The festive opening of Fort Worth Alliance Airport on December 14, 1989, officially launched the fledgling development. Managed by privately held Alliance Air Services, a subsidiary of Hillwood, the airport now features a 9,600 x 150-foot primary runway, direct taxiway access, and a full Category III Instrument Landing System. Alliance offers a foreign trade zone, along with triple freeport inventory tax exemptions and on-site customs.

Attracted by the economic benefits these conveniences would provide, major aviation companies have relocated their facilities next to Alliance Airport. Today, American Airlines operates a $482 million aircraft maintenance and engineering center from its complex. In

American Airlines

During the past decade, a strong partnership has developed between American Airlines and Hillwood. That partnership was launched with our decision to locate a major aircraft overhaul maintenance base at Alliance Airport.

In January 1992, our $482 million maintenance base at Alliance was opened – ahead of schedule and under budget. The state-of-the-art facility quickly became an integral part of American's global maintenance operations. The Alliance corridor is ideally suited to house our maintenance facility due to its close proximity to DFW International Airport and the availability of easy rail and truck access to the business community.

Since its opening, the American maintenance facility has also become home to Texas Aero Engine Services Limited, a joint venture between our company and engine manufacturer Rolls Royce. In addition to American's own aircraft, the maintenance facility now services Rolls Royce aircraft engines from throughout the Americas.

Part of the attraction of Alliance, today, is the extensive array of top companies that have chosen to locate facilities in this unique community. This manufacturing, distribution and business center has generated thousands of new jobs for the North Texas region and many new opportunities for local companies.

American Airlines is proud of its partnership with Hillwood, a partnership that continues to grow with the construction of the American Airlines Center in Dallas. The future is indeed bright at Alliance, and our company is glad to be a part of this unique business community.

Bob Baker
Executive Vice President
American Airlines

Burlington Northern Santa Fe Corporation

The more than $100 million we spent to build our rail hub at Alliance was one of the best investments we have made. The facility has become an anchor for our Southwestern operations.

There are many reasons to locate facilities at Alliance. The development is ideally situated. By utilizing Alliance as the site for our own rail facility, we have significantly reduced transport times to the upper Midwest and the Pacific Coast. In addition, the development's infrastructure is superb and the staff is talented and responsive.

One of the most important factors in our decision to locate at Alliance was the reputation of the Alliance team. They have the ability to draw new industry. That is critical. Their attraction of potential rail customers is helping our business expand.

The rewards, in fact, have been so great that we have seen our rail facility at Alliance grow beyond expectations. We outgrew our intermodal facility shortly after it was completed. Alliance has the resources to allow us to continue to expand and keep up with our growth, which is outpacing both the national and state economies.

The Alliance developers are visionary. They deliver what they promise. They have enabled us to establish a true partnership that has been mutually rewarding.

ROBERT D. KREBS
Chairman and Chief Executive Officer
Burlington Northern Santa Fe Corporation

Nokia, Inc.

Nokia came to the Metroplex in 1992 with a handful of people to manufacture mobile phones in a joint venture with Tandy Corporation. When we outgrew our first manufacturing site, we selected the Alliance corridor as the best place to accommodate our rapid growth, attract a quality workforce and provide good access to world-class transportation hubs.

Today, Nokia is the world's largest mobile phone maker, and our Alliance factory is Nokia's largest manufacturing facility. Combined with our adjacent distribution center, we employ more than 3,100 here—and we're still growing.

Our success has been aided considerably by the strong business climate and good neighbor attitude Hillwood Development has created. We have had a very positive experience and total support from the Hillwood team, and we look forward to many more years of continued prosperity and growth here.

K.P. WILSKA
President, Nokia Inc.

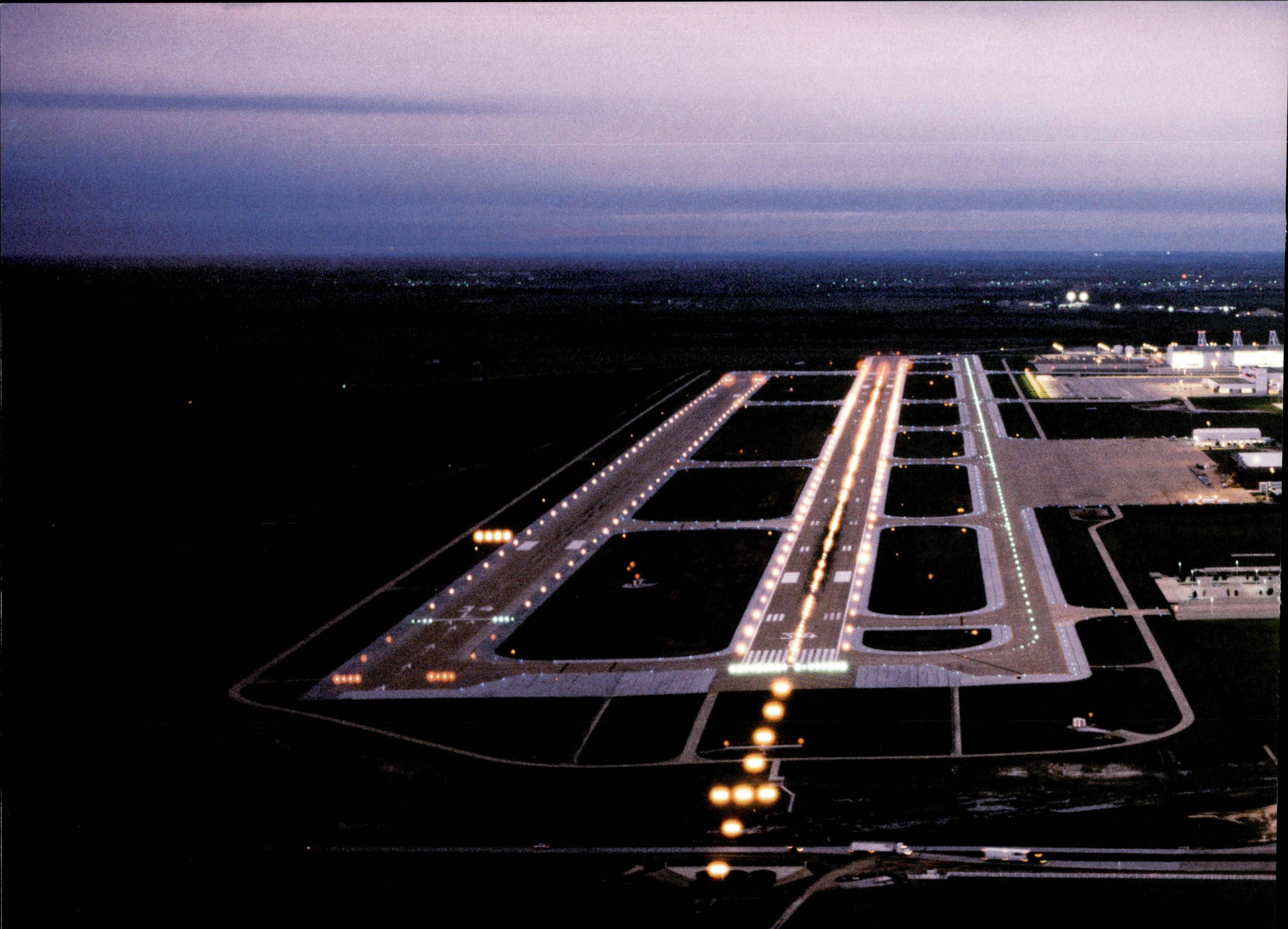

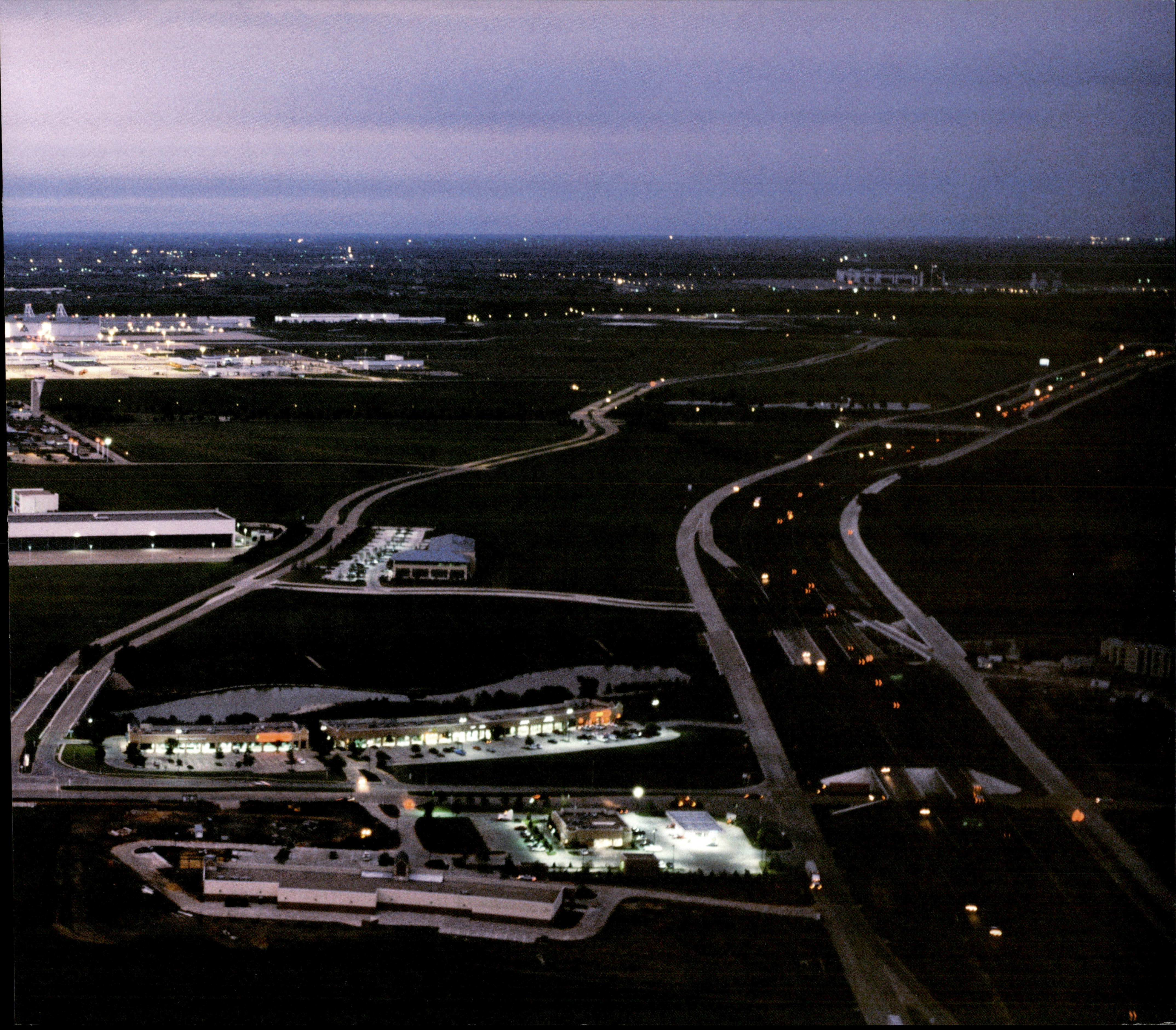

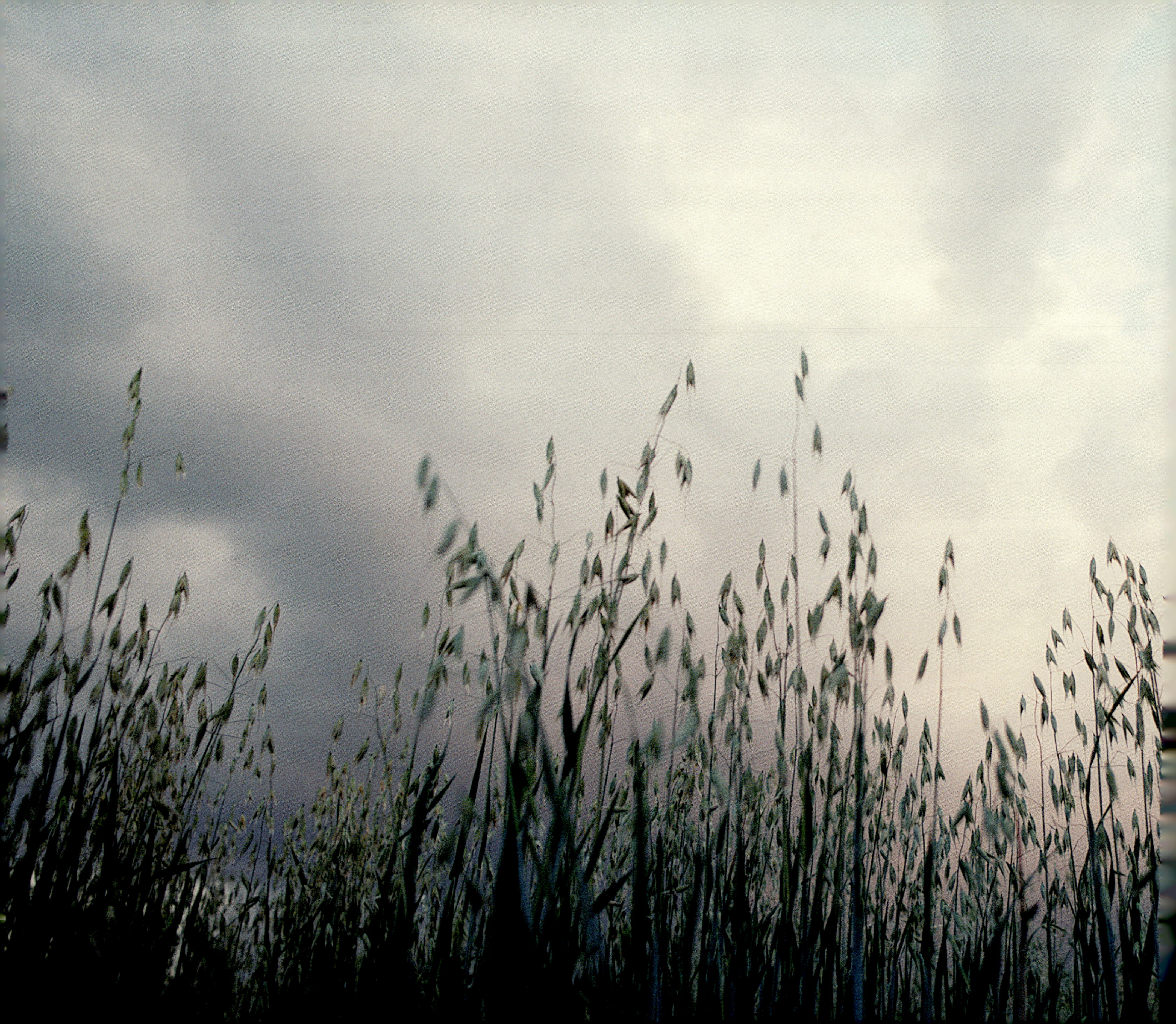

Chapter One The Vision

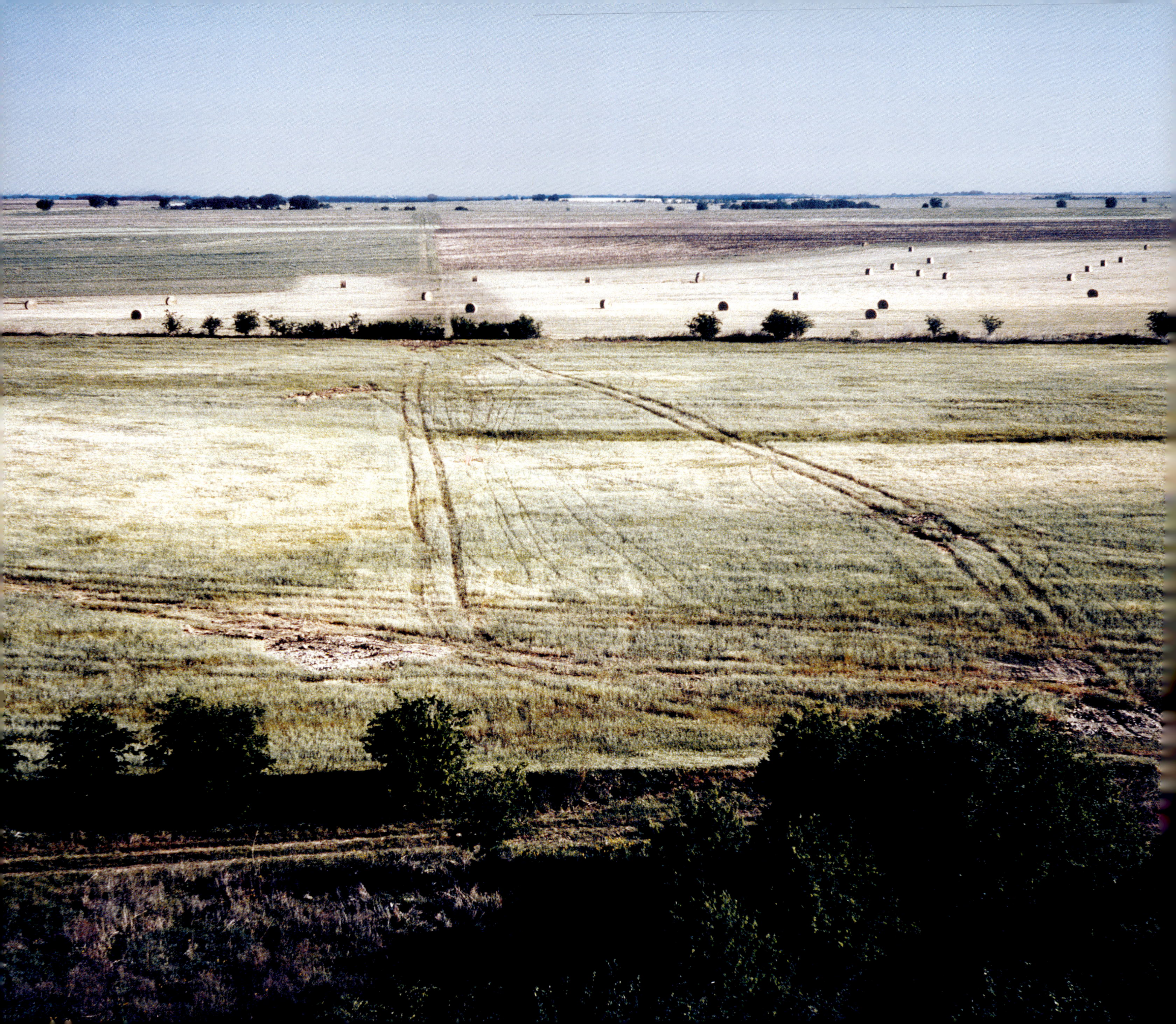

THE VISION 3

It has been more than 150 years since the U.S. Army's 2nd Cavalry Unit established a small outpost on the North Texas prairie. The fort was built to protect settlers from the Indians that freely roamed the surrounding plains. In the intervening decades, that outpost has blossomed into one of the most prominent cities in the nation and the world.

In the early days, it was the promise of opportunity that drew people of every type to this new Western town. Cowboys, cattlemen, card sharks and even a few criminals made their way to Fort Worth, often with nothing more than a vision to guide them. The dedication and perseverance of these pioneers helped transform the settlement into a growing Western city.

Even as the once-thriving cattle markets of the 1800s withered and Fort Worth legends Butch Cassidy, the Sundance Kid and Bat Masterson became fodder for history books, neither the vision nor the growth in this Western town subsided.

Today, a gleaming modern skyline, dominated by structures of steel and glass, has replaced Fort Worth's once dusty streets. Aerospace, finance and manufacturing have become the area's most prominent businesses. And Lexus automobiles are far more common on city streets today than Longhorn steers. Still, through all the changes and growth, Fort Worth has retained the pioneering spirit that was born here 150 years ago. Today, that initiative has launched a new vision that is again changing the North Texas landscape.

Aerial view of the wheat field long before the dream of the Alliance runway was realized.

Flags greet visitors at the entrance of Alliance Airport, the nation's first airport specifically built for industrial and corporate users.

Longhorns still graze in pastures by Alliance Airport.

A New Vision

The growth that transformed the Fort Worth business district during the past century had still not reached the prairies of the northern edges of the city by the mid-1980s. Though less than 15 miles from the city's burgeoning business district, this area was primarily agricultural land.

It took strong, progressive leadership to look across these rolling acres and see the opportunity that was masked by prairie grass. Yet, in the mid-1980s, a small group of business leaders began to consider the future of North Fort Worth. Led by Ross Perot Jr., dreams of a model industrial enclave began to be hatched.

In less than 15 years, those "futuristic" dreams have been surpassed by reality. The Alliance development has forever changed the North Texas landscape. In so doing, it has delivered jobs and opportunity to the Metroplex and unleashed a new era of development for Fort Worth.

At Alliance, the simplicity of nature successfully co-exists with modern technology. Elizabeth Creek, top left, provides a scenic northern border for Alliance. Top right, Workers inside the American Airlines maintenance facility can see ranchers herding their cattle in a nearby pasture.

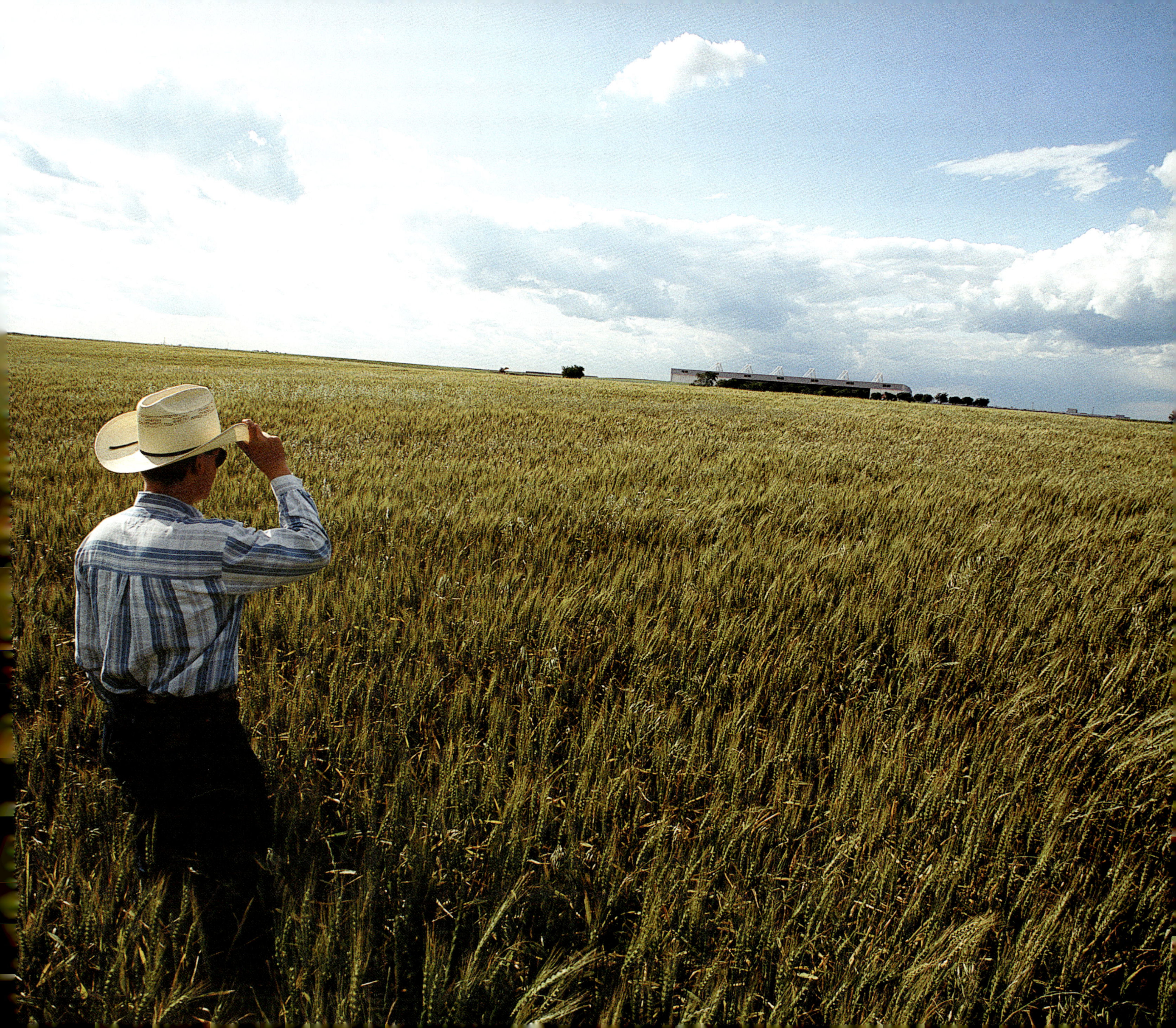

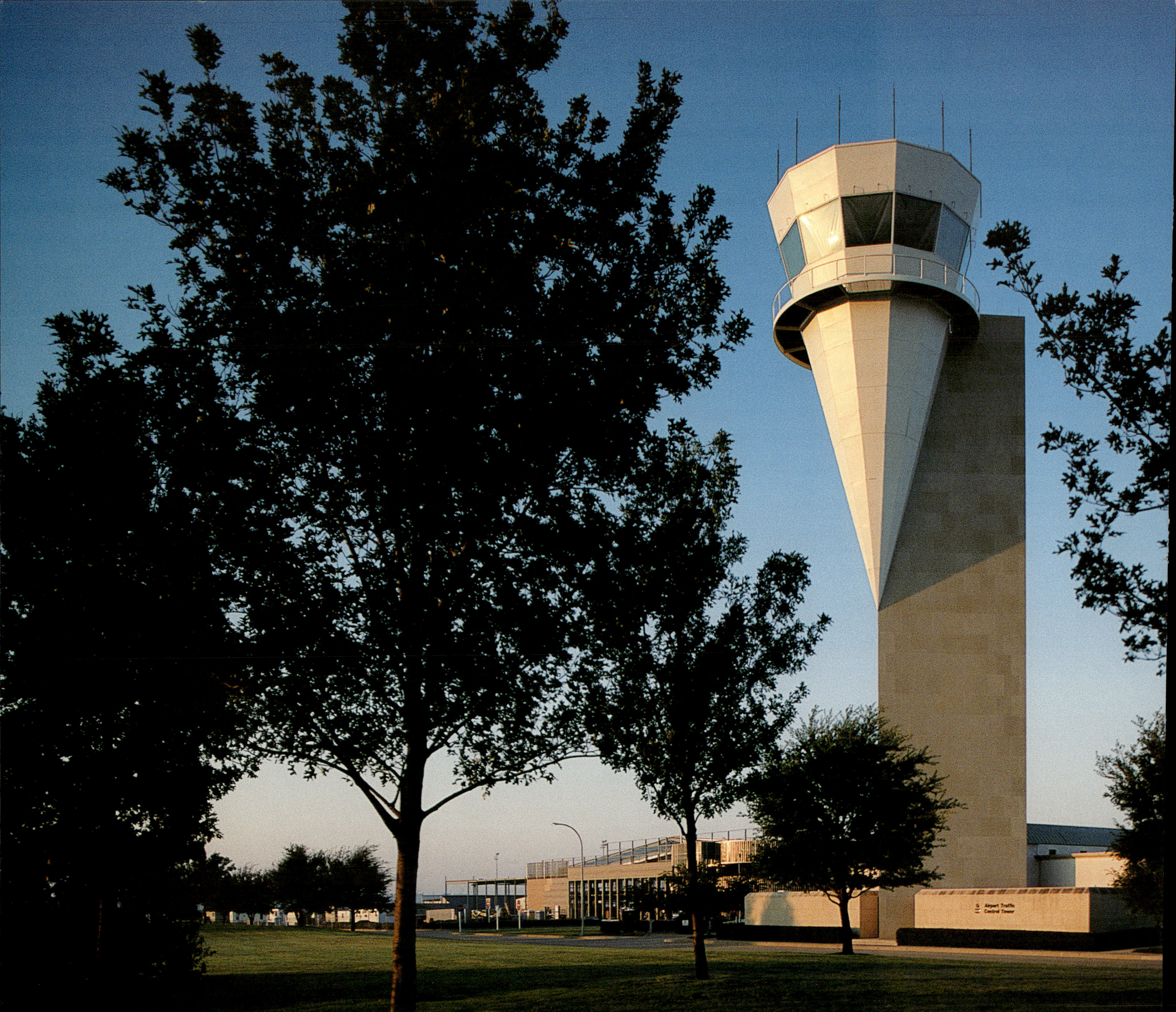
Airport Traffic
Control Tower

The Vision is Born

It was, perhaps, a little-known study produced for the city of Fort Worth in 1964 that provided the first spark needed to launch Alliance. That study predicted the need for a new airport on the northwest side of Dallas-Fort Worth to alleviate anticipated congestion at existing air facilities. By 1985, the Federal Aviation Administration (FAA) began seeking a location for this relief facility. A number of small North Tarrant County cities voiced interest in the project. However, the expansive acreage that would be needed forced the FAA to look to private landholders. Their search led them eventually to Ross Perot Jr.

By this time, Perot had accumulated more than 10,000 acres of undeveloped land in the area and was predicting strong future growth in Tarrant and Denton counties. Still, by Perot's own account, there was no vision for the development of the area. He had begun acquiring land in the region merely as a long-term investment opportunity. The idea of an industrial community clustered around a full-service airport was certainly not on the drawing boards.

Alhough most members of the Alliance team give Perot the credit for generating the Alliance vision, Perot says it was the city of Fort Worth and the FAA that gave Alliance its start. The creation of the airport was simply part of the DFW master plan, which anticipated the need for reliever airports to reduce congestion at the DFW International Airport. His role was merely to "speed up" the process.

Before its development, the Alliance area consisted mainly of wheat fields

This 1988 artist's rendering illustrates the vision of the Alliance team to transform raw land into an inland port.

Completed in 1992, the 24-hour FAA-operated control tower at Alliance Airport has received several awards for its unique architecture.

1989 architectural land plan for Alliance

Perot credits some lesser-known players for the broader Alliance vision, including Gordon Shunk of the North Central Texas Council of Governments that first approached him about donating land for the construction of an airport. Shunk was prompted to contact Perot because of his reputation for providing acreage for such public ventures.

"It was leadership from the public sector that got this project off the ground," notes Perot. He adds that Shunk was the first to suggest the creation of a "cargo airport." The vision was later expanded as Perot discussed the potential project with Dwayne Jose, a former executive vice president with Bell Helicopter Textron. It was Jose, Perot says, who suggested creating a broader "industrial airport," which would provide more development and job growth than a cargo facility.

As with any good piece of history, the "real story" is dependent upon the storyteller. In this case, Jose is quick to offer his own version of events and claims little credit for Alliance. Instead, he says he simply informed Perot that the early plans for the airport were too limited for Bell to seriously consider the facility as a future manufacturing site.

"I didn't actually come up with any ideas," recalls Jose. "I just told Ross that his airport was too small."

Despite these differences of opinion about the Alliance vision, clearly Jose's comments led Perot to consider building a larger airport — one with a runway longer than 9,000 feet that could accommodate aircraft of almost any size.

According to early Alliance team members, Electronic Data Systems Inc. founder Ross Perot Sr. initially discouraged his son from building the airport on his undeveloped land holdings. The senior Perot feared that the noise from the facility would discourage potential tenants.

The development phases of the Alliance Airport runway over the years, from its dusty beginnings on July 9, 1988. Today, the 9,600 x 150-foot primary runway and an 8200 x 150-foot parallel runway are capable of accommodating all types of commercial aircraft to access all global markets.

Early rendering of Alliance Airport

May 1988

January 1989

July 1990

May 1991

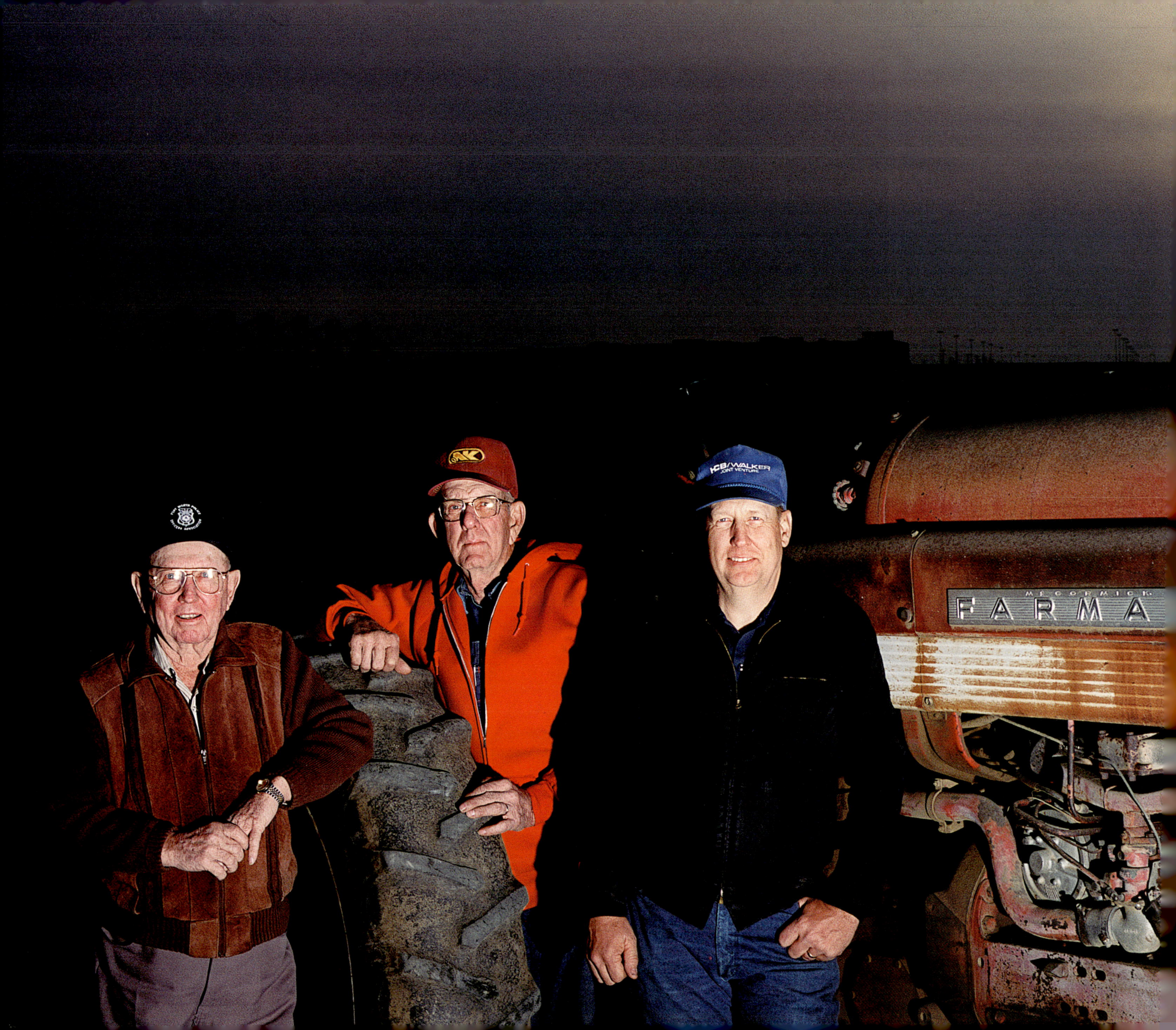
KCB/WALKER
JOINT VENTURE
McCORMICK
FARMA

THE VISION 11

Ross Perot Jr. had already begun to envision an industrial development, however. He investigated the proposal, seeking advice from experts throughout the aviation industry. That investigation eventually convinced both him and his father that an airport straddling the Tarrant and Denton county lines could help spur regional growth and act as a lure to attract companies.

The first shovel of dirt had yet to be turned, but Ross Perot Jr. was already defining the future of Tarrant and Denton counties. On February 13, 1987, newspapers across the country reported that he had offered to donate land for the construction of an airport. The proposed airport seemed to provide the wings necessary to carry the plan forward.

The senior Perot later became one of the most vocal proponents of the Alliance project, referring to the development as an "inland seaport." "All great cities in the past have been built near seaports," said Perot. "Now, cities that aspire to greatness will have to be located near airports connecting them to more diverse ports of call."

Even though it is "painful" to part with land that had been cultivated for over 125 years, the Peterson family sold their farm to Ross Perot Jr. and Hillwood Development so Alliance could become a reality. Pictured on the facing page, left to right, are brothers Howard and Calvin with LeWayne (Howard's son).

Pieces of the Puzzle

Building the framework for the Alliance development was not an easy task. By Perot's own admission, more than 100 transactions were necessary to accumulate the vast real property holdings necessary to make the project a reality. Even as plans for the airport were being crafted, certain key parcels of property were still being acquired. One of those was the Peterson family farm, which represented an essential ingredient in future expansion plans. However, the property had been farmed by the Peterson family for more than 125 years, and it had great sentimental value.

According to Calvin Peterson, the first crops were planted on the property in 1873 by his great-grandfather, who had emigrated from Europe only four years

Harvest time at the Peterson wheat farm consisted of a variety of chores performed by many hands.

earlier. Though it was "painful" to part with the farm land, Peterson came to understand Perot's vision and developed a strong respect for him. Even today, Peterson counts Perot and Hillwood Chief Legal Officer David Newsom, who worked closely with Perot on the acquisition, among his personal friends. In 1988, with the acquisition of a section of Peterson's farm, Perot pieced together the essential elements necessary for the Alliance development.

Today, Peterson visits the property regularly, as he has for decades. In fact, he is such a regular to Hillwood's Alliance office that the company provided him with his own coffee mug. And while others see new buildings and progress at Alliance, Peterson helps remind them about how the property once appeared. He is proud to point out, for example, that the planned Intel manufacturing plant is located "in the middle of the oat patch."

Acquiring the Peterson farm was a mixed blessing for Perot and Newsom. While it provided the land necessary to expand the development, they found themselves missing the home-cooked meals the Peterson family used to prepare during the lengthy contract negotiations.

A portion of the Peterson farm remains today. The future Intel plant site is in the background.

Dub Blessing, longtime Perot associate, enjoys a friendly chat with Calvin Peterson.

Busy road construction workers get Alliance ready for growth.

The Foundation

Even before the announcement that Perot had offered to donate land for the construction of an airport in Fort Worth, the foundation for a Texas-size industrial and commercial development was being laid. In July 1986, Perot, Nelson Bunker Hunt and McGuire-Thomas donated the land necessary for the construction of Texas Highway 170 and improvements to connecting Highway 114. The construction of Highway 170 was a "pivotal" milestone in the development of Alliance. The new

A 2-lane road served commuters before Highway 170 was built on the southern side of the Alliance development.

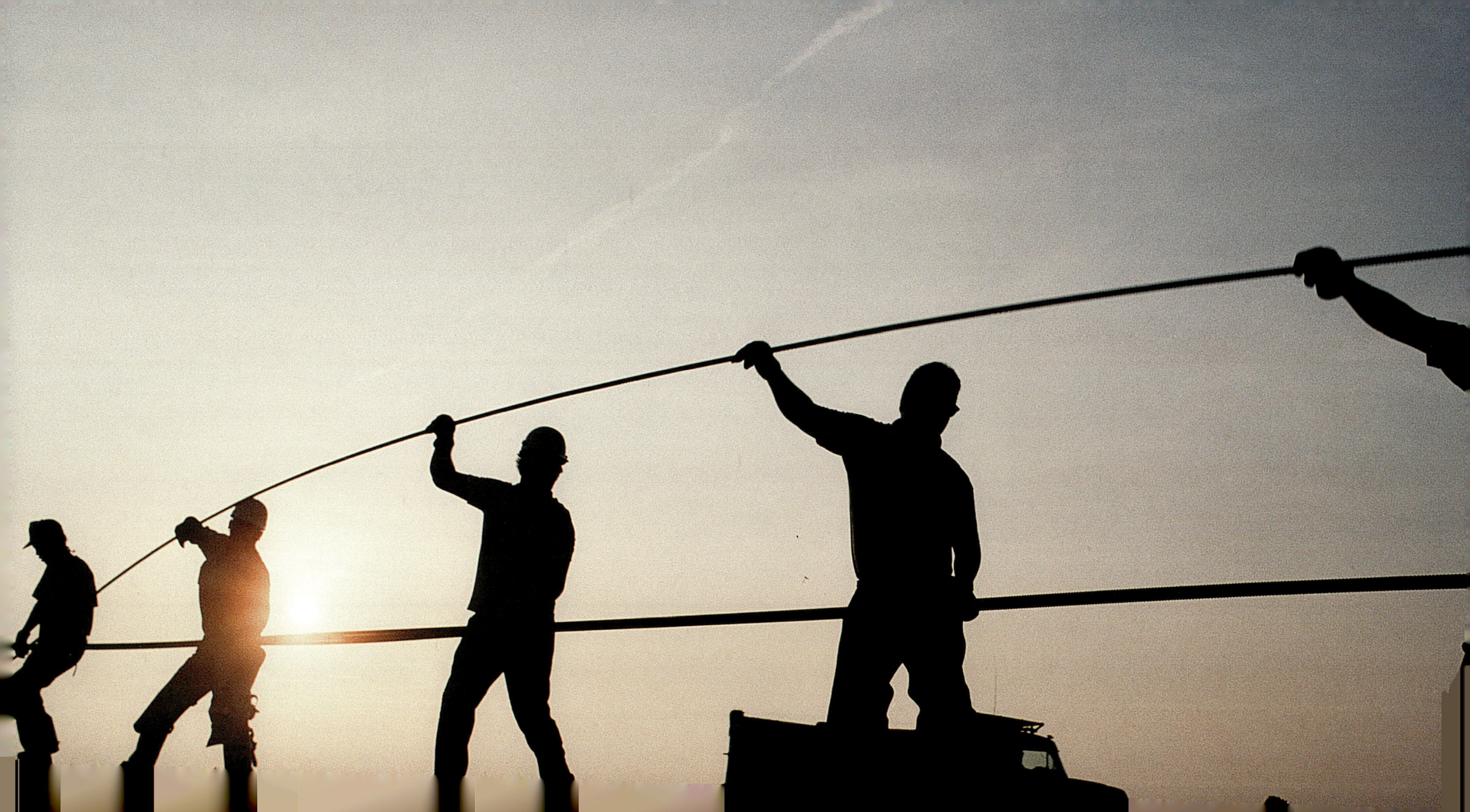

THE RIGHT PLAN AT THE RIGHT TIME

Alliance is the only master-planned industrial airport in the world. When it was launched, the concept of such a multimodal transportation, industrial and commercial hub was virtually unknown. It took more than a vision to transform the idea of Alliance from concept to reality.

"All the stars were aligned," according to Isaac Manning, president of Hillwood Strategic Services. It is true that the conditions were right for the development to prosper.

Ironically, it was bad news that may have provided the motivation necessary for the birth of Alliance. The economic downturn of the late 1980s left many people suffering. As Hillwood's Chief Executive Officer Rick Patterson recalls, the North Texas economy was at a low point, and business and political leaders were looking for a solution at the time the project was conceived. Fort Worth's leaders of the day seized upon Alliance as a prime vehicle for creating jobs and jump-starting the sluggish economy.

By 1987, office vacancy rates in the Metroplex were reported to be among the highest in the nation. Prices for real property had dropped by 10 to 20 percent. Absent such economic motivation, the necessary political coalition may have been more difficult to forge.

In addition to the economic downturn, severe reductions in federal defense spending fell particularly hard on Fort Worth. As U.S. Representative Kay Granger recalls, the city lost more than 50,000 "good paying jobs" during this period. With the defense industry providing 30 percent of Fort Worth's jobs at that time, such losses were devastating.

"Bell and Lockheed were laying off thousands of employees," according to Granger, who served as Fort Worth's mayor during some of the defense cutbacks. "We only had two things to sell: an abundance of skilled employees looking for jobs and Alliance. This was one of the things that saved us."

Additionally, the project required broad support. Accordingly, it was vital to have leaders in place at the local, state and national levels that had the foresight to see the opportunity presented by the development itself. Such leadership was offered by former Fort Worth Mayor Bob Bolen, the Fort Worth City Council, former Speaker of the House Jim Wright, former U.S. Representative Pete Geren, FAA officials and others. The result has been the creation of more than 14,000 jobs in a decade.

While the Alliance team was able to find the right recipe for success, that mix has eluded others. Even as the ground was being broken on the Alliance airport facility, T. Allan McArtor, the former chief of the FAA, was predicting the development to start a wave of similar projects. He boasted that the U.S. needed "a dozen Alliance airports."

Meanwhile, the Alliance team is the only group to have been successful in building such a project. The development continues to be viewed as one of the premier industrial and commercial developments in the world and a model.

It may not be statistics of job growth and investment that provide the greatest evidence of the success of the unique venture, however. For some on the Alliance team, the evidence came in the words of a single construction worker. Ross Perot Jr. led a group that was surveying the airport site soon after construction had begun. Of course, the recession had eliminated many North Texas jobs and there was not a lot of hope among local residents.

As the group crossed the airport site, a construction worker walked up and thanked them, adding that he would not have a job without the project. At that moment, early team members understood the enormity and importance of Alliance.

road would provide direct and easy access between the Alliance development and DFW International Airport.

Still, turning Highway 170 from a dream into a reality would be a great challenge. The working partnership between Alliance developers and public agencies was vital to the highway project's success, according to Hillwood CEO Rick Patterson. In order to make the highway seem more feasible to state highway department officials, the Alliance team collected land along the highway's proposed path, offering it to be used for the road. Hunt provided additional acreage for the project, and the Alliance team donated engineering and design services.

Through the donations of land and services, the Alliance team was able to reduce the cost of the project for state agencies and raise it on the construction priority list. However, the Texas Department of Transportation had already realized the potential growth such a highway could provide in Tarrant and Denton counties.

In addition, a strong partnership had been built between the city of Fort Worth, the FAA, former Speaker of the U.S. House of Representatives Jim Wright and Alliance developers. By 1987, Fort Worth leaders had also begun to realize the potential for growth along the city's northern boundary. The Alliance project was the impetus needed to launch that growth. In April of that year, the city annexed the land upon which Alliance rests today.

"Tarrant County was the No. 1 county in the U.S. for job losses," notes Perot. "They needed something to kick-start the economy. Alliance was such a project. When times are tough, that's when big projects like this get off the ground."

Even as the project was moving ahead on multiple fronts, Perot and the early Alliance team began reconsidering their own vision. In May 1987, the vision of the modern Alliance development was hatched, when Perot announced that his team would seek to expand the airport facility from a $4 million, small commercial facility to a $24 million state-of-the-art airport. Suddenly, both private and public sector leaders were considering a development that could generate tens of thousands of jobs.

Highway 170 would "pave the way" for the success of Alliance, providing easy and direct access to and from DFW. Eventually, 170 will extend westward to connect with FM 156.

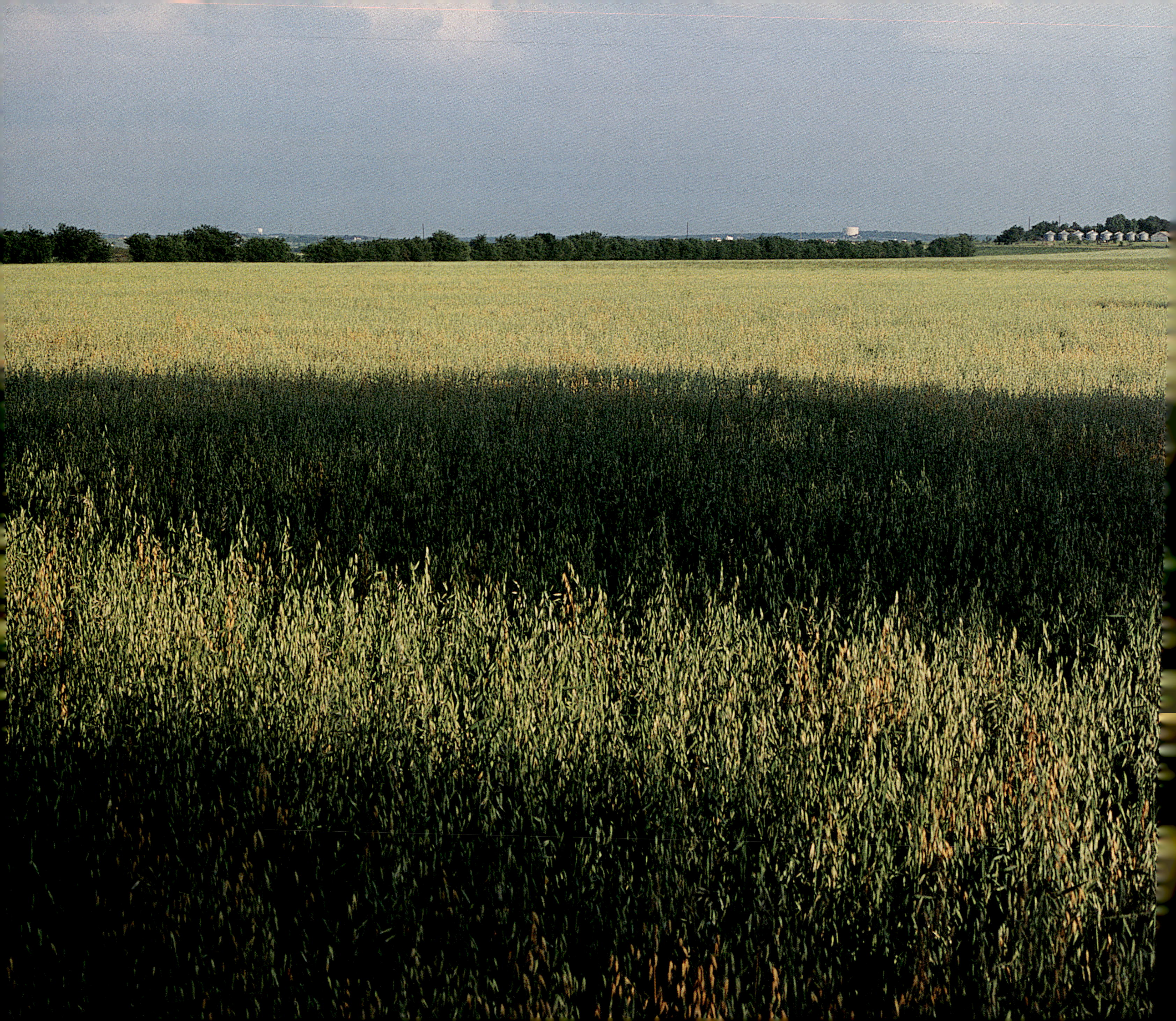

Chapter Two Breaking Ground

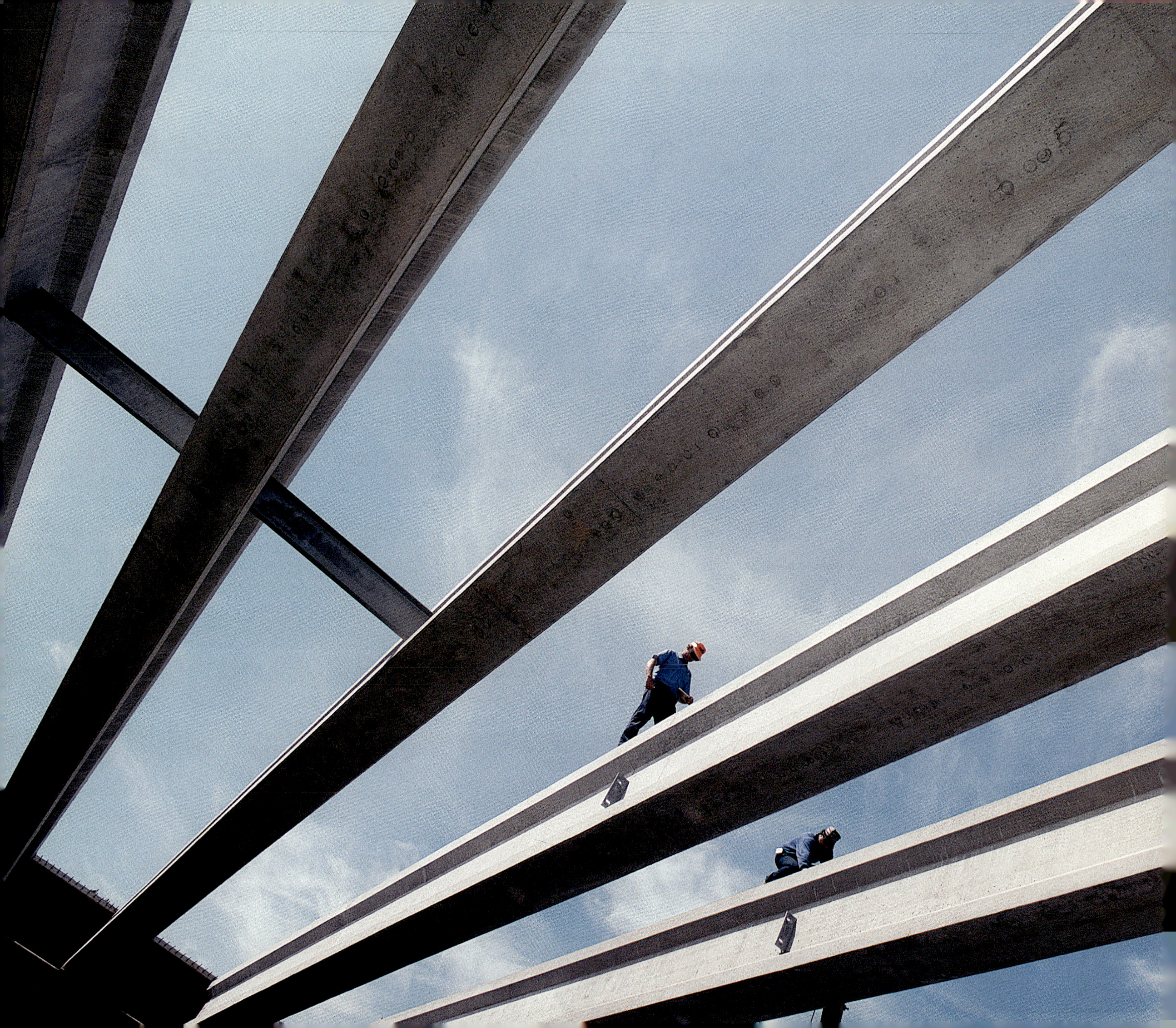

For the small Alliance team that had been assembled by the end of 1987, New Year's Eve had special meaning. It was, indeed, a time to respectfully usher out the old and welcome the opportunities that lay ahead. However, for them, the old and the new were represented in a large tract of land stretching across Tarrant and Denton counties.

On a brisk and cloudy afternoon, the members of the early Alliance team rented horses and rode the full perimeter of the property that would soon house a world-class industrial center. It was their last opportunity to say goodbye to the pristine prairie that rolled across the North Texas landscape. They knew that the very face of the land would soon change.

Led by Perot, the group was seized by a sense of excitement. It had taken tremendous work to give birth to the Alliance vision. Soon the vision would begin to take physical shape. Silently, as they rode, they welcomed the future of this area.

Ross Perot Jr. invited the public to a barbecue picnic following the groundbreaking of the U. S. Engraving and Currency Plant in North Fort Worth. On the future Alliance property, he announced plans for the new airport. Former Speaker of the U. S. House of Representatives Jim Wright (right) is on hand to address the informal gathering.

Perseverance

Looking back at those early days of the development of Alliance, Hillwood Strategic Services President Isaac Manning, who helped fine-tune the unique master plan, attributes Perot's perseverance and determination with keeping the project alive. In fact, he admits, there were occasional, fleeting moments of doubt even among team members.

"I remember flying over the property with Ross Jr. before it was developed," recalls Manning. "He would say, 'We're flying over the runway now.' We'd look out at the pasture and say, 'Sure.'"

The Alliance development has room to expand across open pastures, such as this one.

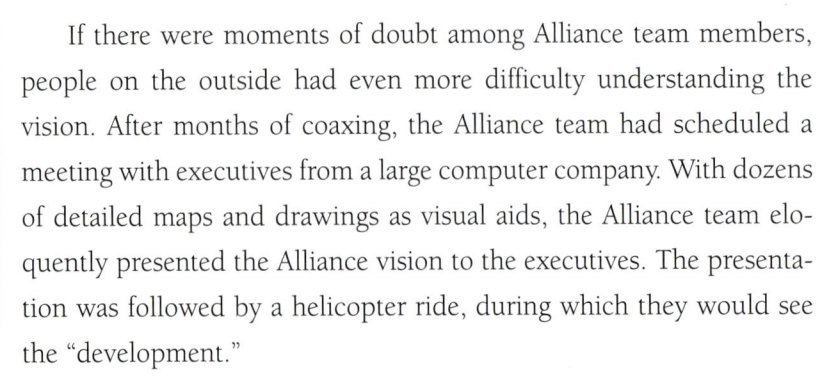

If there were moments of doubt among Alliance team members, people on the outside had even more difficulty understanding the vision. After months of coaxing, the Alliance team had scheduled a meeting with executives from a large computer company. With dozens of detailed maps and drawings as visual aids, the Alliance team eloquently presented the Alliance vision to the executives. The presentation was followed by a helicopter ride, during which they would see the "development."

Pointing to the maps, Perot described the runway design and other development features as they flew over the vacant prairie.

"We were talking about the runway and buildings, and all these guys could see were cows. They kept looking and looking for the runway," recalls former Hillwood executive Frank Zaccanelli. "They thought there would be actual structures, but they didn't see anything. They left thinking we were a couple of fruitcakes."

Alliance Advanced Technology Center press conference.

Kenneth Barr, mayor of Fort Worth, speaks during Ameritrade announcement in council chambers.

Teamwork

However, it was not just Perot who persevered through these often trying times. The Alliance team put forth extraordinary effort to keep the surrounding communities informed and enthused about the project through the good and bad times. This was vital to the success of the project.

Meanwhile, team members worked hard to spread information about the development.

"People were surprised about how much direct contact we had with them on this project," said Robyn Kelly, who was a big part of the outreach program. "We went into the communities to tell our story. We were at meetings, community events and bake sales. We even gave our home phone numbers out to area residents. By keeping residents informed directly, we avoided a lot of misinformation."

Artist's rendering of control tower

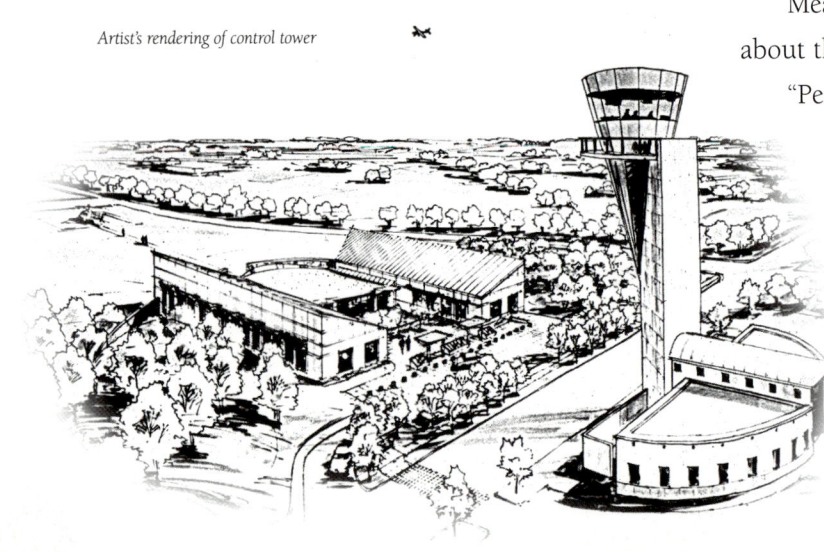

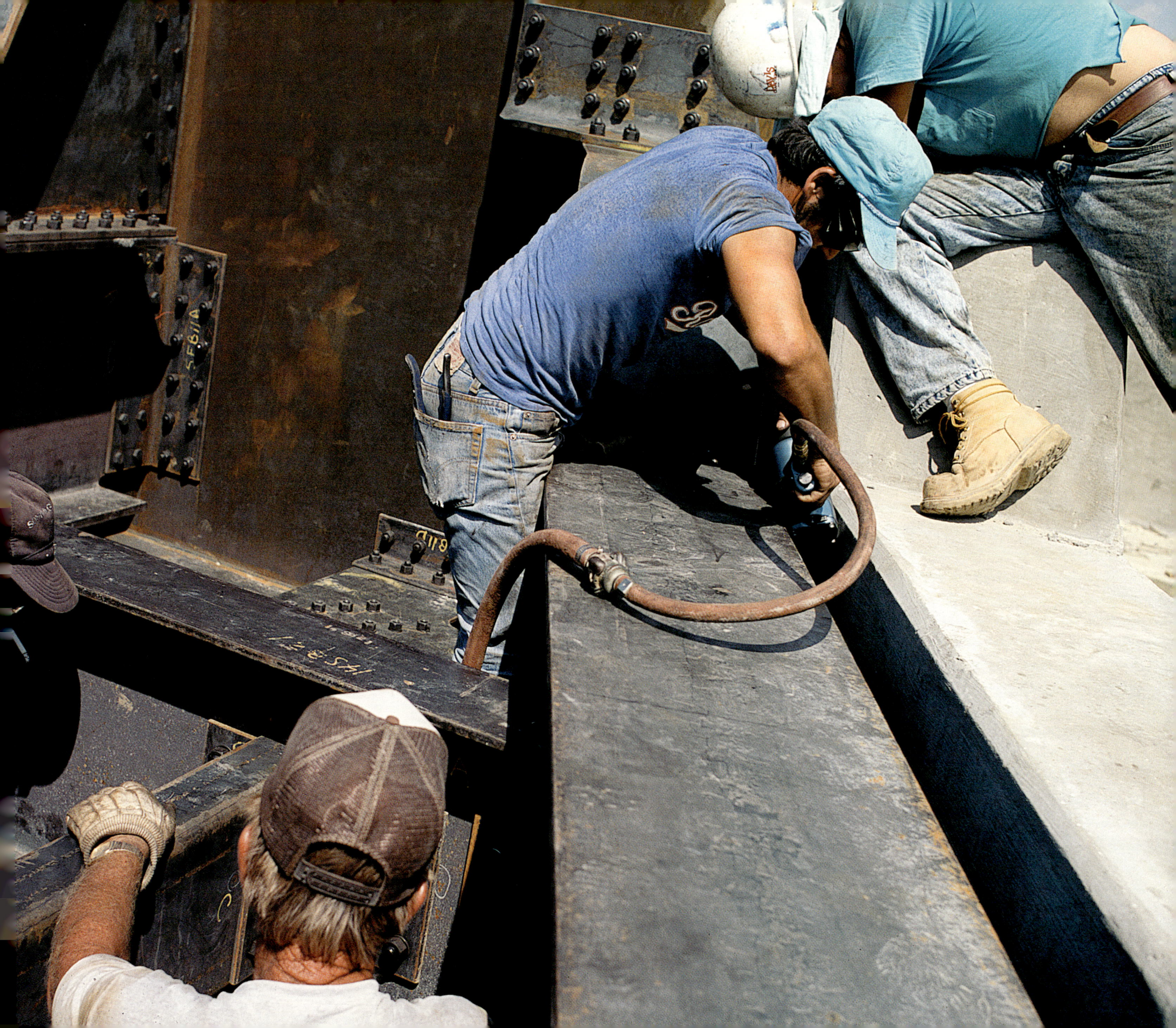
Davis

A TRUE PARTNERSHIP

As the project founder, Ross Perot Jr. credits the unique partnership between the public and private sectors with transforming the Alliance vision into reality. It was, indeed, a unique example of cooperation.

While numerous representatives of the FAA played a role in crafting the Alliance vision, it was then Speaker of the U.S. House of Representatives Jim Wright who provided significant support for the project in Congress. In addition to securing support for the $24 million in federal funding needed for construction of the airport, Wright also helped author legislation creating rules for the establishment of "industrial airports" within the FAA regulations.

"The leadership of Bob Bolen and Jim Wright helped us cut through years of red tape," according to Perot. Absent the strong leadership provided by these individuals, Perot speculates that the airport project may have been delayed by years. Instead, it was completed in "record time."

One of the people who worked closely with Mayor Bolen and Fort Worth City Council members was former Alliance team member Frank Zaccanelli. He recalls that the relationship between these groups was not always hospitable. In fact, Zaccanelli describes the early days as being "almost adversarial." Bolen has similar memories.

"I recall telling Frank that I had only thrown three people out of my office in my entire career, and he was two of them," Bolen jokes today.

Still, a strong bond developed from those early trials. City officials and Alliance team members began to realize the potential scope of the project. The Alliance team became zealots about creating jobs, a tax base and economic development. Perot gives significant credit to members of the Fort Worth City Council, who continued to support the project through numerous "difficult" early votes. "They were able to stay focused on the long-term potential," notes Perot, adding that their early visions of the project have been vindicated in terms of real job growth and economic development.

Though many of them were not around to see it, the fruit of the work of these early council members is evident today. In addition to thousands of new jobs created, the Alliance project has generated $59 million in tax revenues for the city of Fort Worth, Tarrant County, Northwest Independent School District, Denton County, the city of Haslet and the city of Roanoke.

By 1990, this partnership had become so strong, then President George Bush pointed to the Alliance development as a national model for public/private partnerships. This recognition provided substantial early credibility for the project and enhanced early marketing efforts.

Since then, the partnership between the public and private sectors has remained strong. Others playing a critical supportive role in the construction of Alliance have been former U.S. Rep. Pete Geren, current U.S. Rep. Kay Granger, Texas Governors Mark White, Ann Richards and George W. Bush, Fort Worth Mayor Kenneth Barr and a multitude of others.

Above: Intel announces its plans for Alliance at Fort Worth City Hall.

Below top: Former Fort Worth Mayor, Bayard Friedman, a Japanese dignitary, former Governor Ann Richards and Ross Perot Jr. at North Texas Commission conference.

Below bottom: Fort Worth Mayor Kenneth Barr.

Below left: 1989 Fort Worth City Council: Back row, left to right: David Chappell, Steve Murrin, Eugene McCray, Louis J. Zapata, William Garrison; Front row, left to right: Kay Granger, Garey Gilley, Mayor Bob Bolen, Virginia Nell Webber. Below middle: Former U.S. Representative Pete Geren. Below right: Ross Perot Jr. and Kay Granger.

Mike Berry, president of Hillwood Properties, addresses a group at Alliance.

Of course, the contacts included more than appearances at meetings. During one period the Alliance staff made personal calls to every person in the Haslet phone book.

Several early members of the Alliance group cite Perot's emphasis on teamwork as a central factor in the success of the project. Staffers had no titles and very little hierarchy. In fact, members did not even have business cards until sometime in the early 1990s. The informal atmosphere enabled the Alliance staff to work more effectively as a team.

The bond, fostered by Perot's management style, helped the Alliance staff form closer relationships and believe that they could accomplish the impossible. Looking back on that early staff structure, Fort Worth Chamber of Commerce Executive Vice President Bill Thornton refers to Perot as a "pacesetter."

1991 Alliance team members include, left to right, Richard Squires, Tim McCabe, Isaac Manning, Bill Burton, David Hardesty and Mike Berry.

"Ross was very intentional in building a cohesive staff structure," notes Thornton. "Today, theorists point to this style of leadership as a revolutionary model for the corporate world to adopt. He was doing this more than 10 years ago."

An Opportunity

The other ingredient necessary in keeping the vision of Alliance alive in the early years was the foresight of Fort Worth's leaders. Former Mayor Bob Bolen and members of the city council looked at the fledgling development as an opportunity for Fort Worth to continue to grow. Even as the economy sagged locally, these leaders realized the untapped resource available in the form of vast, undeveloped prairie to the north. House Speaker Jim Wright played an instrumental role in securing funding for the airport facility.

Former Speaker of the House Jim Wright speaks at the Alliance Airport opening on December 14, 1989.

A spectacular air show celebrated the Alliance Airport groundbreaking in July of 1988.

In fact, it was the cooperation and partnership struck between the city of Fort Worth, the FAA, state and federal officials and the Alliance team that led to the development's name. It was during lunch one day that Perot's sisters, Suzanne and Nancy, first offered the name "Alliance," noting that the word aptly described the union of the various entities involved in the development.

The name stuck and was adopted by the Fort Worth City Council in May 1988, just weeks after the FAA approved the federal grants necessary for the construction of the expanded airport.

Accompanied by aircraft of every size and shape, a U.S. Air Force skydiving team and the Texas Air National Guard band, ground was broken on the Alliance airport on July 10, 1988. Yet, even the groundbreaking ceremony proved challenging. The first challenge involved planning an air show at a facility that did not yet exist. Perot recalls making requests for Air Force jets, military personnel and other aircraft to be part of the show. He received many skeptical responses when he explained that the airport, the site for the planned event, had not been built.

A second challenge involved directing the aircraft to the proper location. The Alliance team came up with the idea of lining the proposed runway strip with bulldozers. This solution allowed aircraft pilots to identify the location of the future runway and the airshow to proceed on schedule.

Looking back on that period, Sharon Rae, an early member of the Alliance outreach group, recalls Perot's confidence and his unusual formula for success.

"We'd face setback after setback. In every case, he'd figure out a way to overcome the roadblocks. Usually, the solutions didn't involve high-paid consultants or experts. It was just common sense."

With the groundbreaking accomplished, the Alliance vision had taken another major step toward reality. The future pace of development would be dizzyingly swift.

At the official spade-turning are, left to right, Odie Cowart, the former mayor of Haslet; T. Allan McArtor, former FAA administrator; Bob Bolen, the former mayor of Fort Worth; Jim Wright, former Speaker of the U.S. House; and Ross Perot Jr., chairman of Hillwood.

Brightly colored hot-air balloons delight visitors during an Autumn Balloon Festival.

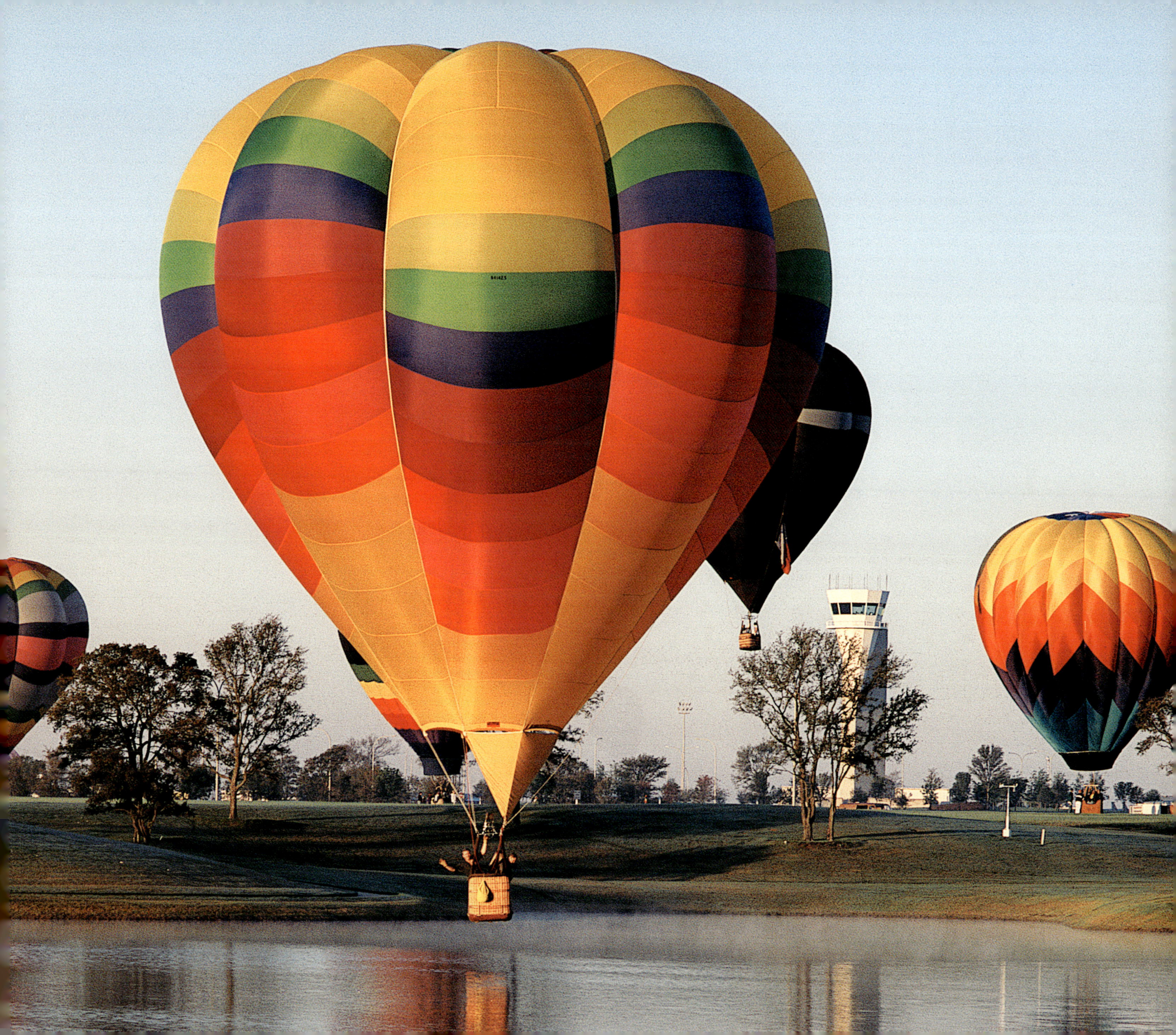

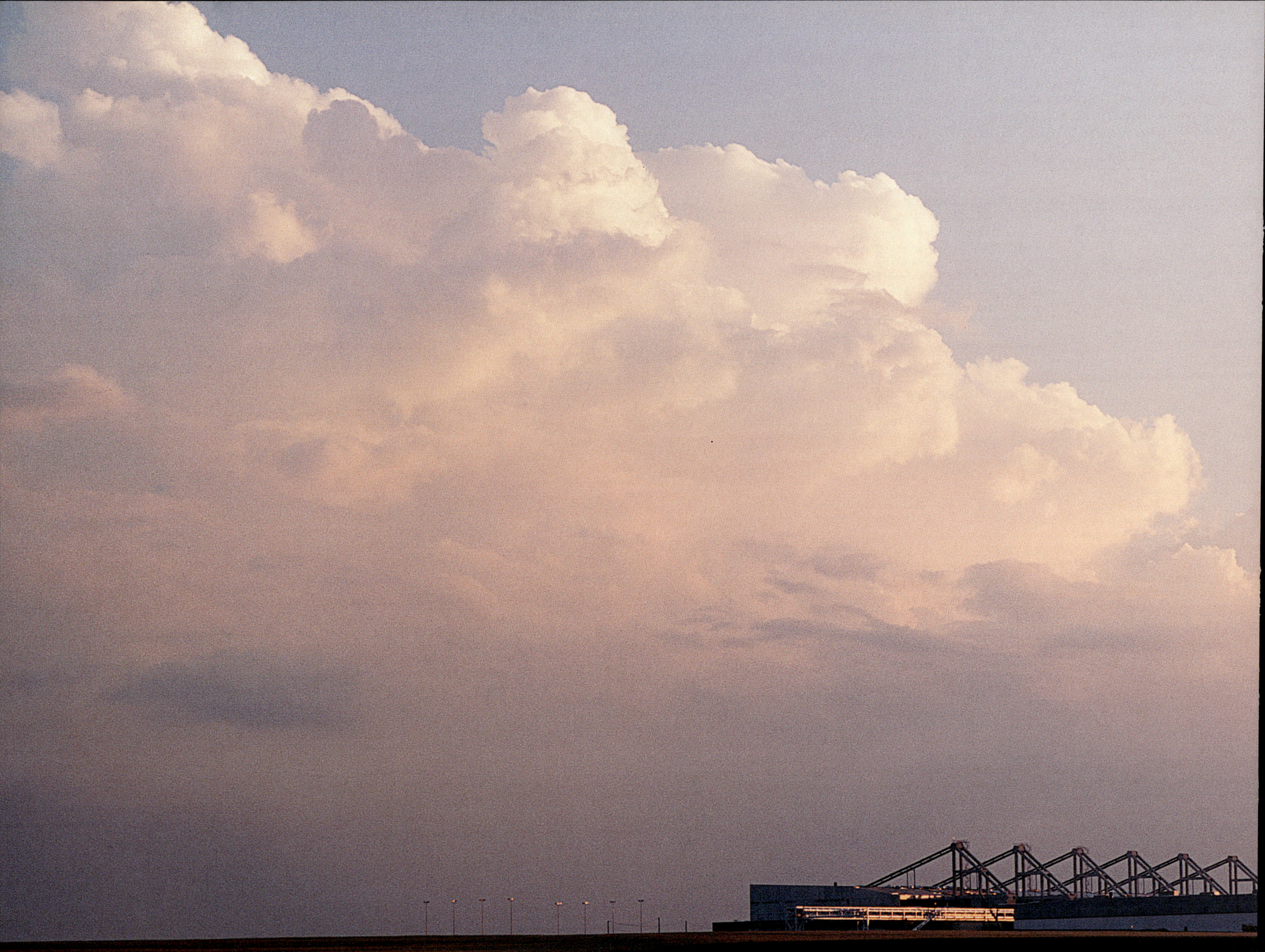

Chapter Three The Vision Takes Shape

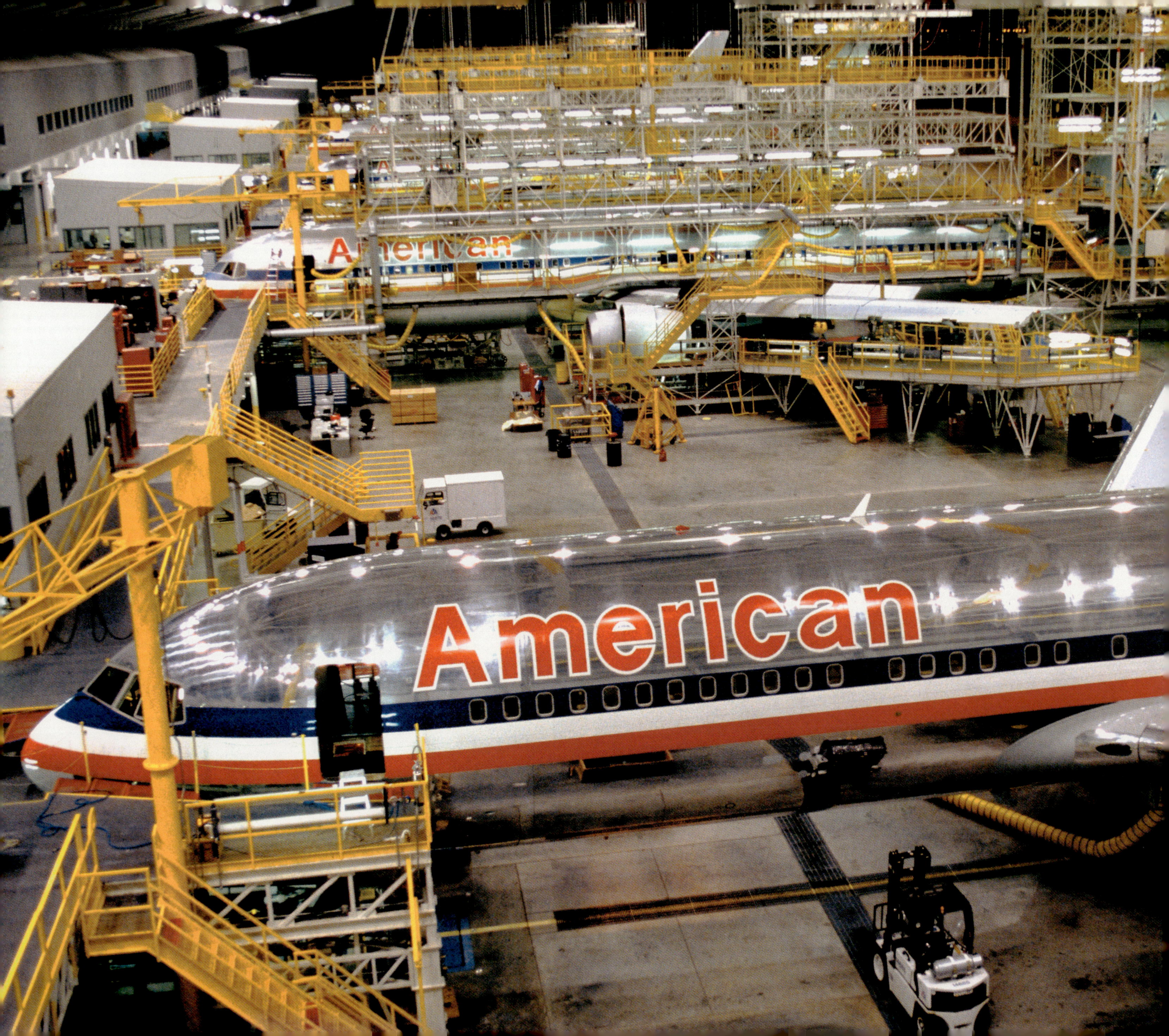
American

THE VISION TAKES SHAPE

Marketing had become the key task for the Alliance staff by early 1989. Though the Alliance airport facility had barely been started and no tenants had been signed, the marketing team found itself wooing two major prospects: Santa Fe Railway and American Airlines. Mike Berry, president of Hillwood Properties, and others on the team had the responsibility of selling a vision that few could fully comprehend.

The team adopted what Berry terms a "proactive" marketing strategy. "We had to make things happen. We had to take advantage of every opportunity and be aggressive," Berry recalls.

Their aggressive tactics started with the American Airlines deal. The Alliance planners feared being cut from American's short list in early 1989. Since the airport was not yet complete, American officials were believed to be questioning the practicality of choosing the Alliance facility as a company maintenance base. Accordingly, Berry and Perot put together an "11th hour" trip to visit with American Airlines executives in Tulsa, Oklahoma.

Late in the evening prior to the morning meeting, Berry was struggling for a strategy that would communicate the team's interest in the American project. During these waning evening hours, he had the idea to make a sign stating, "Welcome to the future home of American Airlines." At Berry's request, the team rushed to get the sign made and placed it prominently alongside the future airport runway.

The American Airlines maintenance facility offers a colorful light display at night.

Former Fort Worth Mayor Bob Bolen, right, joins former American Airlines CEO Bob Crandall to announce his company's move to Alliance in June of 1989.

Left: In June of 1989, American Airlines locates its $482 million maintenance and engineering facility at Alliance, housing the largest single cantilever building in the world.

American Airlines now employs over 2,000 workers at Alliance.

AN INTERVIEW WITH FORMER MAYOR BOB BOLEN

As mayor of Fort Worth, Bob Bolen played a key role helping to create the Alliance vision. He provided the leadership necessary to build support for the project and to guide essential legislation through the city council. Yet, he admits that the project was not always easy to sell to constituents or colleagues. Still, he notes the long-term potential for growth the development offered for Fort Worth made the project a vital tool in the city's recovery.

Question: The Alliance vision grew and changed over time. When was the modern vision for Alliance first communicated to you, and what was your first reaction?
Bolen: I never heard the long-term vision initially. The truth is that we didn't know what was going to happen. I've been surprised by the success of the project. I think Ross was also. The distribution warehouses and all of the other new pieces were never articulated at the beginning. What has resulted is the first industrial airport of its kind in the world. The concept was new and untested. The results have been great for Fort Worth.

Question: This vision of an industrial airport was a new concept. How difficult was it to build support for the project?
Bolen: Very few people understood the vision initially. It was very difficult in certain cases. Fort Worth is very conservative. We are willing to pay the price for development, but we are selective about the projects we support. I was certainly criticized about this project by some. My philosophy was always that if you create good jobs, this solves a multitude of social ills. I felt like this project had the potential to do that.

We tried to get one-of-a-kind prospects at Alliance. We wanted businesses that would not upset a competitor across the street. We also looked for companies that would draw in supplemental businesses—suppliers and parts manufacturers. We have now created 14,000 jobs out there. It has proved to be a tremendous success.

Question: You worked closely with Ross Perot Jr. and the Alliance team in turning the project from dream into reality. Was it difficult in maintaining the bond between this private group and the various public players?
Bolen: The FAA had been trying to get an airstrip out there for years. We didn't have the money to build another airstrip. At City Hall, we are only facilitators. If it were up to us alone, we would probably still be waiting. We decided we should let him do it, if he was willing.

Ross is a tremendous driver. That was the way he was brought up. His dad taught him that if there is a hill, he was either going over it or through it. He was also very generous with his time and effort. He was willing to be part of the community.

We are bound by a lot of regulations at the city. I could not legally take the kinds of risk with city funds that I would take with my own money. I would not want to. When we turned this project over to Ross, it got done twice as fast as we could do it and for less money. This project was simply a great example of the ways in which the public and private sectors can work together.

Question: Were there ever strains in the relationship?
Bolen: Was it easy? No. Were they hard negotiators? They were. They pushed us pretty hard at times. As part of the private sector, they did not always understand the constraints we had. There were always some in the public who disagreed with the project as well. That is always true. Despite the strains, it never took long and we were working together again. We were lucky that they only wanted first-class facilities. They were not just after a quick profit.

Question: The Alliance vision has been reshaped several times over the years. Still, the project has grown remarkably fast. Looking toward the next decade, what does the future hold for this development?
Bolen: I believe the future is going to be far different than we think it will be. I do believe the scale of the project provides a great advantage. Alliance has the critical mass that a small developer could never have.

I am not sure where the next deal will be. I do know the project will be more focused on issues relating to the quality of living. I believe we will see health-care facilities out there and continuing education opportunities. If you look 10 years ahead, I think you are talking about growth we cannot even envision now.

Berry and Perot flew to Tulsa the next morning and picked up the American executives. On their way back to the Fort Worth project site, Berry began to worry that the sign had been too aggressive. Negotiations were still confidential and the sign, he feared, would generate unwanted attention. However, he knew it was too late to remove the sign. Fortunately, it had no negative impact on the deal. Perot recalls that American Airlines officials laughed about it at first. However, their laughter was followed quickly by a single request: "Hide the sign."

As Berry recalls, the team was not so lucky when the tactic was employed a second time. A similar sign was posted as the Russian airline Aeroflot visited the Alliance facility for confidential negotiations relating to the establishment of their own cargo center. With a chuckle, Berry notes that the sign was photographed and appeared in area newspapers, much to the chagrin of the Aeroflot executives. He admits the tactic has not been used again.

Enterprise zones, a foreign trade zone, a user fee airport, an on-site customs office, a freeport tax exemption, and a world trade center attract companies of all types to Alliance.

A Special Tool

While the Alliance marketing team utilized some unique tactics, it was a single piece of equipment that became their most essential tool: the helicopter. As Mike Rosa, Fort Worth Chamber of Commerce vice president, recalls, the helicopter allowed the Alliance team to display the direct connection between the project and other critical developments throughout the region.

During a brief helicopter ride, prospective tenants were able to personally experience the proximity of Alliance to DFW International Airport, downtown Fort Worth and major industrial centers

Future customers regularly survey potential sites for their operations.

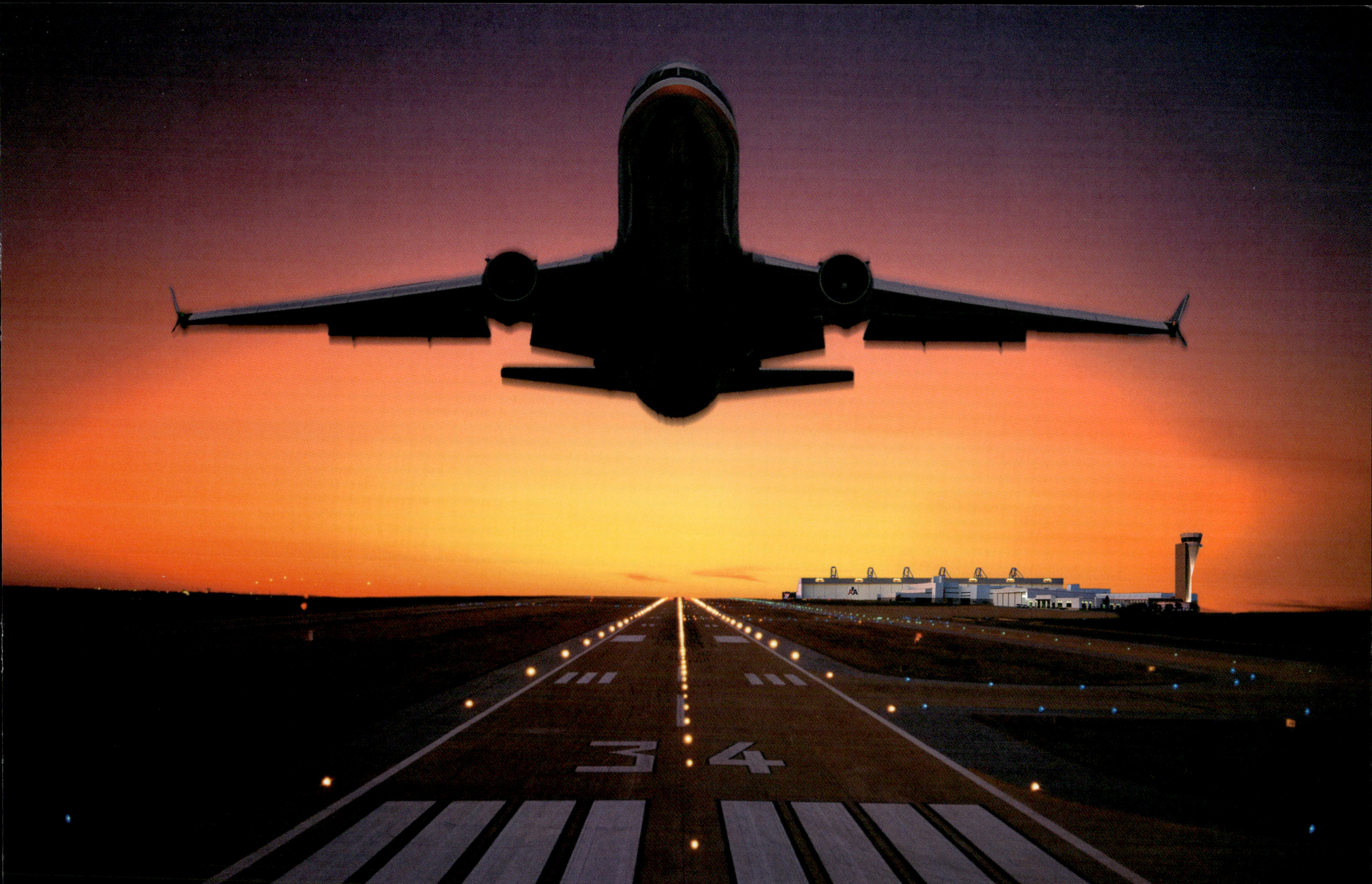
34

Prospective customers prepare to enjoy a bird's-eye view of Alliance via helicopter.

located throughout the Metroplex. As Rosa notes, Alliance team members did more than show prospective clients an area map. They put those clients "into the map."

It was not just prospective Alliance tenants who responded to this unique airborne tour. U.S. Rep. Kay Granger recalls that she was first introduced to the Alliance vision aboard Hillwood's helicopter. At the time, Granger was chair of Fort Worth's zoning commission.

"It was 1986 when Ross called me and said, 'I have something I want to show you,'" says Granger of her first flight over Alliance. "We were flying over fields and cows, and Ross was pointing out where buildings would be located. He was so enthusiastic about the project, I never doubted it would work."

Yet, any tool can have its limitations, as Perot himself soon discovered. Following a board room presentation to several executives from a Japanese company, Perot offered them a helicopter ride. After settling into the helicopter, one executive became agitated when Perot assumed the controls. As the craft became airborne, the executive panicked and tried to grab the controls.

"This guy was screaming," recalls Perot with a laugh. "I guess we scared a lot of people when I climbed into the helicopter as the pilot." He adds, "The Japanese company did not buy anything."

A New Vision

As negotiations continued with American Airlines, an event occurred that changed the direction of the Alliance vision — again. Previously, development plans had centered on the aviation industry. Then, in May 1989, Santa Fe Railway announced its intention to locate a major auto-shipping yard at Alliance and became the development's first customer. This unexpected tenant opened potential new transportation options for future

Burlington Northern Santa Fe Railroad operates an 55-acre auto unloading facility at Alliance. The sale of the land for the auto-shipping yard in May 1989 was the first deal at Alliance.

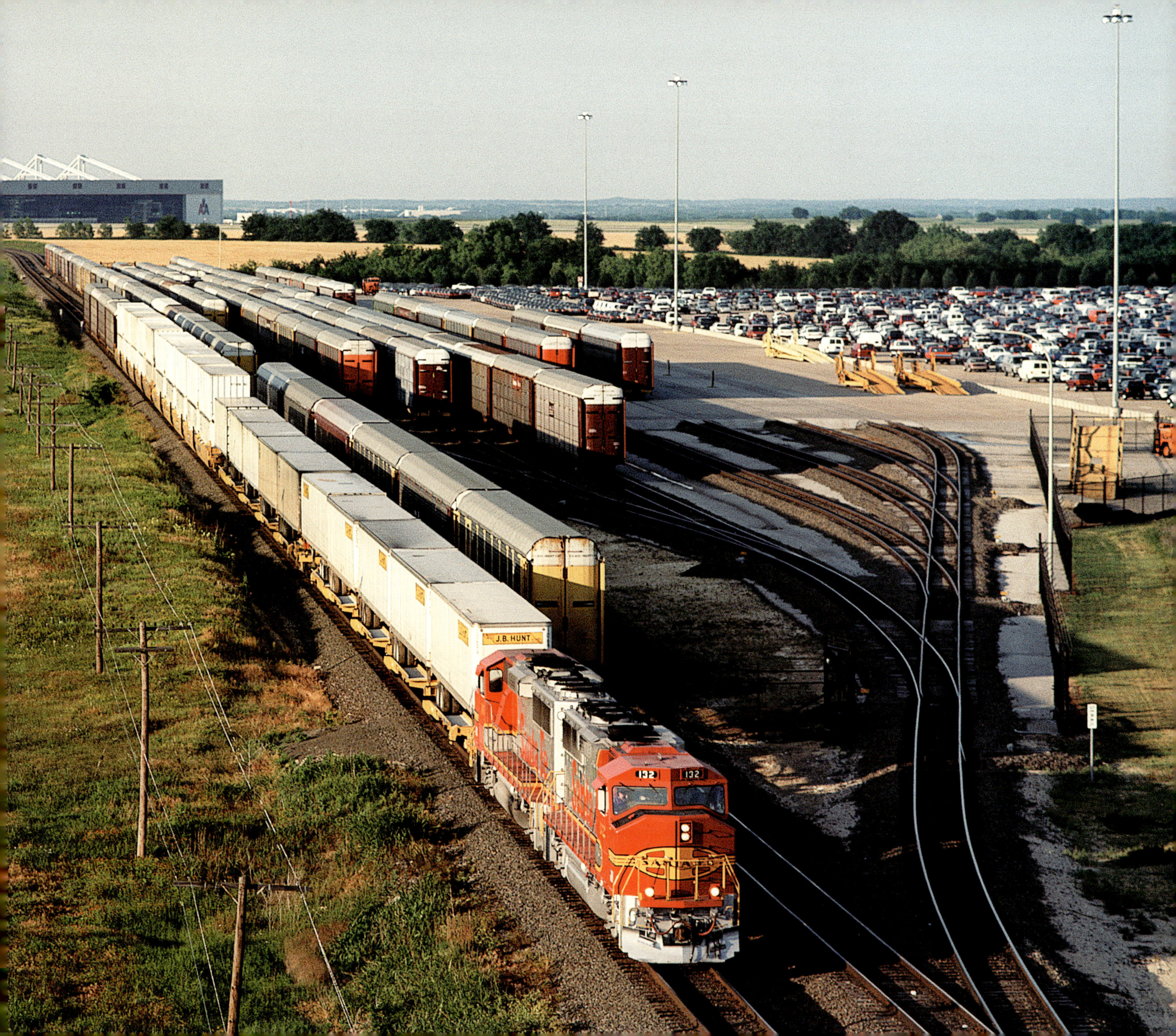
J.B. HUNT
132
132

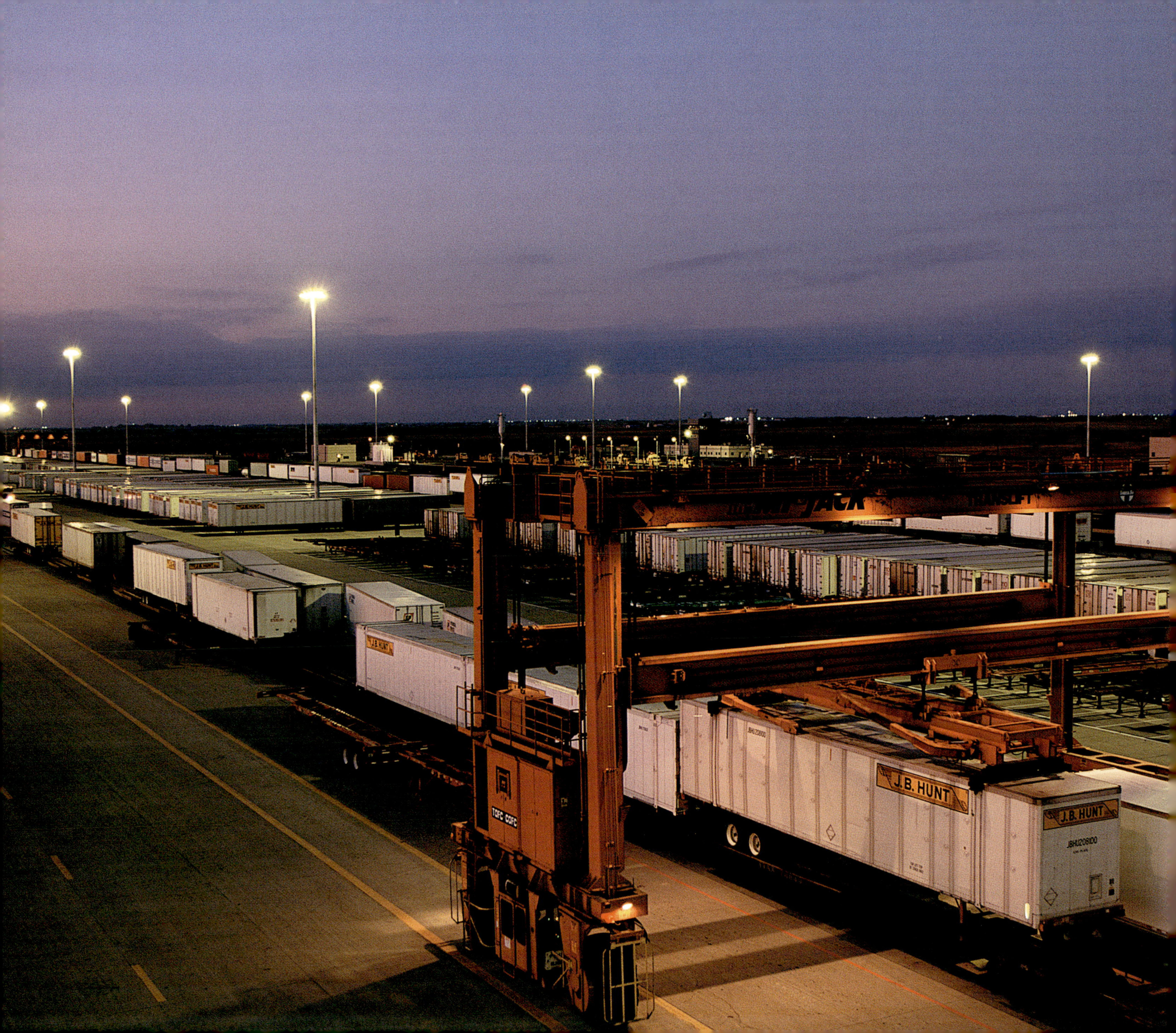
J.B. HUNT
J.B. HUNT
TOFC COFC

customers. Moreover, it changed the facility into a true multimodal transportation hub.

"Santa Fe was really the leader in creating the modern Alliance vision," notes Patterson. "When they decided to come to Alliance, we realized we had more than an airport. We had a major transportation hub."

With the addition of the Santa Fe facility, the Alliance team realized that opportunities were much broader than had been initially envisioned. Santa Fe provided state-of-the-art rail access on the western side of the development. Union Pacific, the nation's largest rail carrier, already had tracks on the eastern edge of Alliance. In addition, Interstate 35W, which bisects the Alliance development, offered the most heavily used commercial automotive route between the U.S., Mexico and Canada. The vision of a true "inland port" was beginning to take shape.

While it was surprising to most that the first Alliance tenant was a railroad company, Perot recalls another point of irony stemming from that early transaction. The parcel of property on which the Santa Fe rail hub sits was, in Perot's mind, the property that would be the most difficult to sell. He admits to being pleasantly shocked that the parcel was the first to be acquired.

Within a couple of weeks, American Airlines made its much-anticipated announcement that it would locate a maintenance base at Alliance. The $482 million facility would generate 2,000 jobs. Though the airport had yet to be finished, the fledgling development had landed two substantial clients within a month. Equally important was the visibility gained by Alliance from these announcements.

"In 1989, the American Airlines deal was the largest aviation facility to be launched in the world," recalls Berry. Indeed, the Alliance airport facility had sprouted wings with the announcement.

Above: Burlington Northern Santa Fe engines sport a new paint job.

Right: Robert Krebs, then Santa Fe CEO, speaks at the January 1993 groundbreaking for the intermodal facility.

The intermodal facility makes up a huge portion of Westport, a 1,200-acre development designed for companies requiring immediate rail access.

Burlington Northern Santa Fe operates one of the largest intermodal yards in the country at Alliance.

CHAPTER THREE

THE INTERMODAL CENTER

For area companies, Burlington Northern Santa Fe's intermodal hub offers a transportation alternative that is both economical and efficient. Intermodal shipping involves the movement of freight using more than one method of transportation. This gives companies the freedom to move products long distances at less cost.

Intermodal shipping uses special containers that can be loaded onto trucks, railcars or steamships. Shippers can then move products from their starting point to their destination without ever having to unload goods or change receptacles. When this feature is combined with different methods of transportation to reach markets around the globe, companies can significantly reduce bottom-line transportation expenses.

By far, Alliance has the most superior transportation network available in the nation. Major highways bisect and surround the project, making shipping by truck a viable way to move goods quickly and efficiently. The Alliance airport serves as an international industrial airport that enjoys the advantages afforded by enterprise zones, foreign trade zones, and a customs office on-site. Rail service is facilitated by Burlington Northern Santa Fe and Union Pacific; both have transcontinental rail lines within the project.

January 1993   *July 1993*   *June 1994*

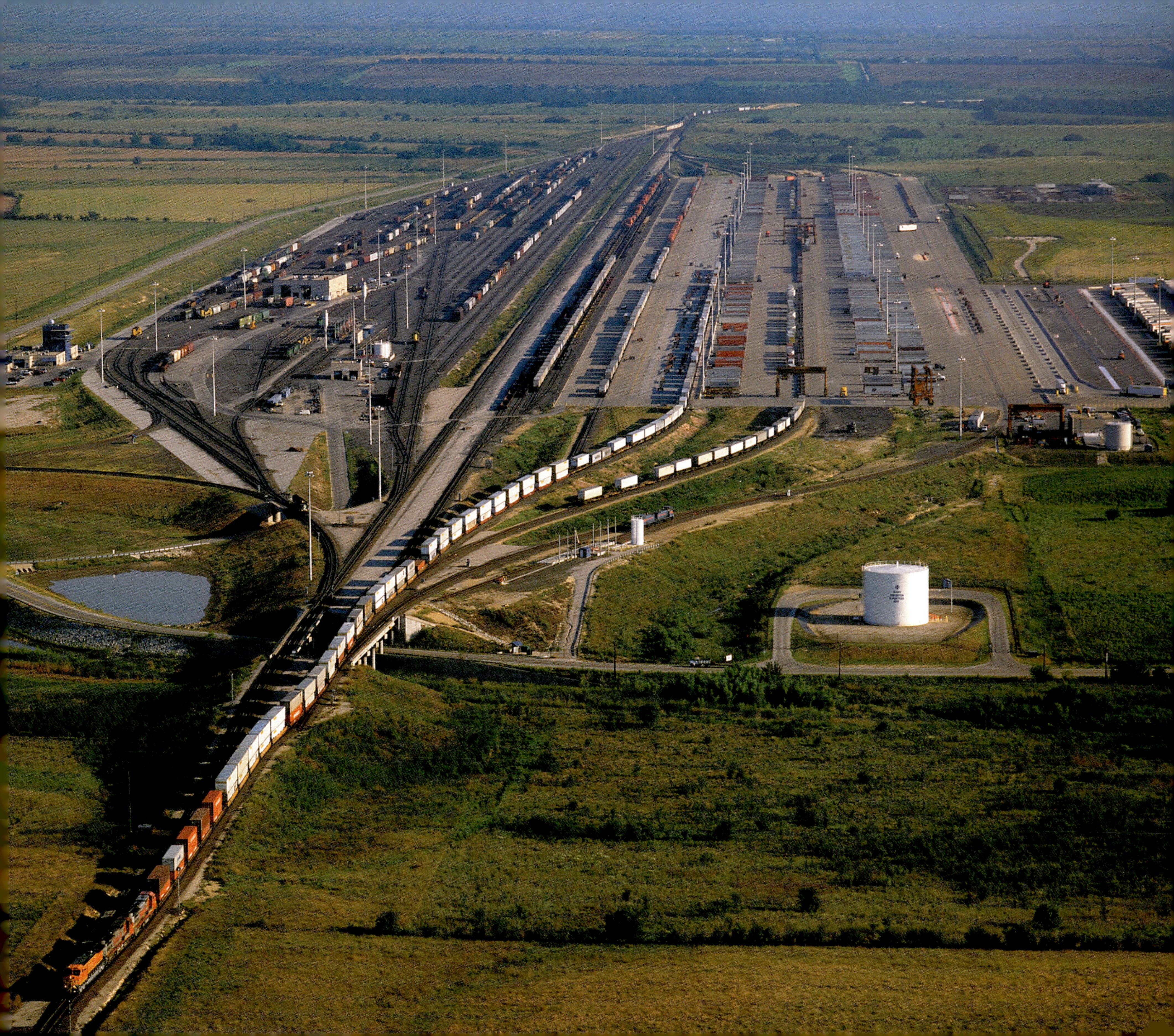

Opening Day

There would be an additional celebration in December 1989, as the Alliance airport facility was opened. Though members of the Alliance team never seemed to fear dreaming the impossible dream, the American Airlines deal had given them new confidence. They displayed their confidence in opening the airport. With work only 75 percent complete on the facility in October, the date of December 14 was selected for the airport opening. The task seemed impossible to complete in such a short time, but team members pulled together and finished the facility not just on time, but in record time, according to Tim Ward, president of Alliance Air Services. On December 14, an airport dedication party was thrown in a tent on the finished airport runway.

The cheers over these developments on the aviation front would dim quickly, however. Shortly after the opening of the new airport, the Berlin Wall came tumbling down and the defense sector of the aviation industry entered a serious downturn. In fact, Richard Squires, one of the very first Alliance team members, notes that the very future of the development looked "dicey" during this period.

"There was a very long lull after the American Airlines deal," recalls Squires. "Business was really slow. Ross had the foresight and the ability to keep the team together during this period. That kept us going."

Despite the drought in new tenants, Perot recalls that he never doubted the Alliance vision would work. "We were on a mission. We believed in this project. If we had known then what we know today, we may never have started."

As the aviation industry struggled to rebound, the Alliance team went to work seeking new opportunities. With construction of the new Texas Highway 170 well underway by the fall of 1990, the Alliance team again reshaped the vision by landing its first distribution center.

The entire community celebrated the opening of the airport in December of 1989.

Former Fort Worth Mayor Bob Bolen accepts the Airport Operating Certificate from former Speaker of the U.S. House of Representatives Jim Wright.

Former Fort Worth Mayor Bob Bolen and former Speaker of the U. S. House of Representatives Jim Wright follow Santa Claus down the ramp after the ceremonial landing of the American Airlines' jet.

On December 14, 1989, an American Airlines' jet became the first to land at Alliance Airport, signaling the opening of the world's first industrial airport.

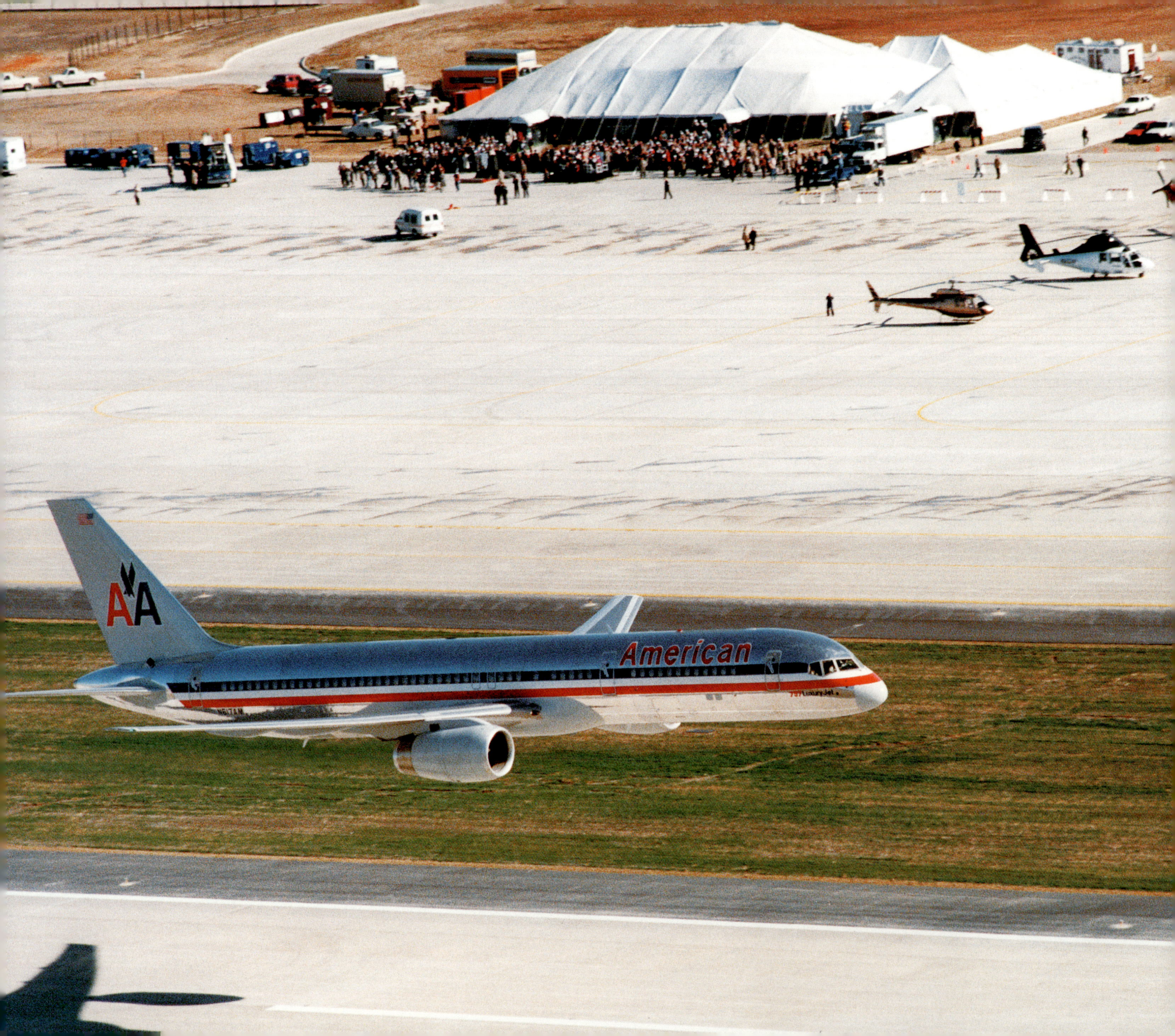
AA
American

In 1990, Hillwood opened the Gateway sector of the development with the sale of 128 acres to Food Lion for a regional distribution facility.

A superior highway transportation network facilitates distribution to and from Alliance.

In September, Food Lion announced plans to build what is now the largest facility at Alliance. The announcement was followed by Nestlé's decision to open a distribution facility at the development. These twin decisions opened an entirely new category of potential growth.

Dreams and Reality

In 1990, the Alliance development also attracted the FAA as a customer. Though not large in scope, the deal became a lasting symbol of the can-do attitude that was prevalent among Alliance team members. FAA officials had planned to locate their new flight standard district office at another site. However, plans had to be scrapped at the last minute when technical problems made the proposed space inadequate. FAA officials then came to Alliance seeking a 5,000-square-foot office ready for occupancy in 60 days, according to Ward.

Alliance team members did not let their lack of available office space interfere with the deal. After agreeing to house the FAA facility, they located modular office units and created office space that's still in use today.

The early work done to create the Alliance project consisted of more than marketing and construction. It also involved dreaming. The Alliance team wanted to provide a distinctive image for the community. They began crafting that image with a design competition in 1987 that resulted in the creation of the unique control tower that stands watch over the Alliance runway.

In 1989 Manning helped direct a second phase of planning aimed at refining the community's distinctive image. Five of the best-known architects in the world were brought to the development for a "dream team" summit. These individuals helped to craft long-term design and land management strategies. At the top of their list of recommendations, according to Manning, was to let the former ranch "be a ranch." In response to this suggestion, the Alliance team has maintained the feel of the rolling prairie that surrounds the development.

The "dream team" summit created a land management model.

Right: In 1994, Nestlé, the world's largest food company, opens a 520,000-square-foot $20 million distribution center on 42 acres in Alliance Gateway, employing approximately 220. The facility handles more than 1,000 food and beverage products, coordinating shipments to outlets in a five-state area.

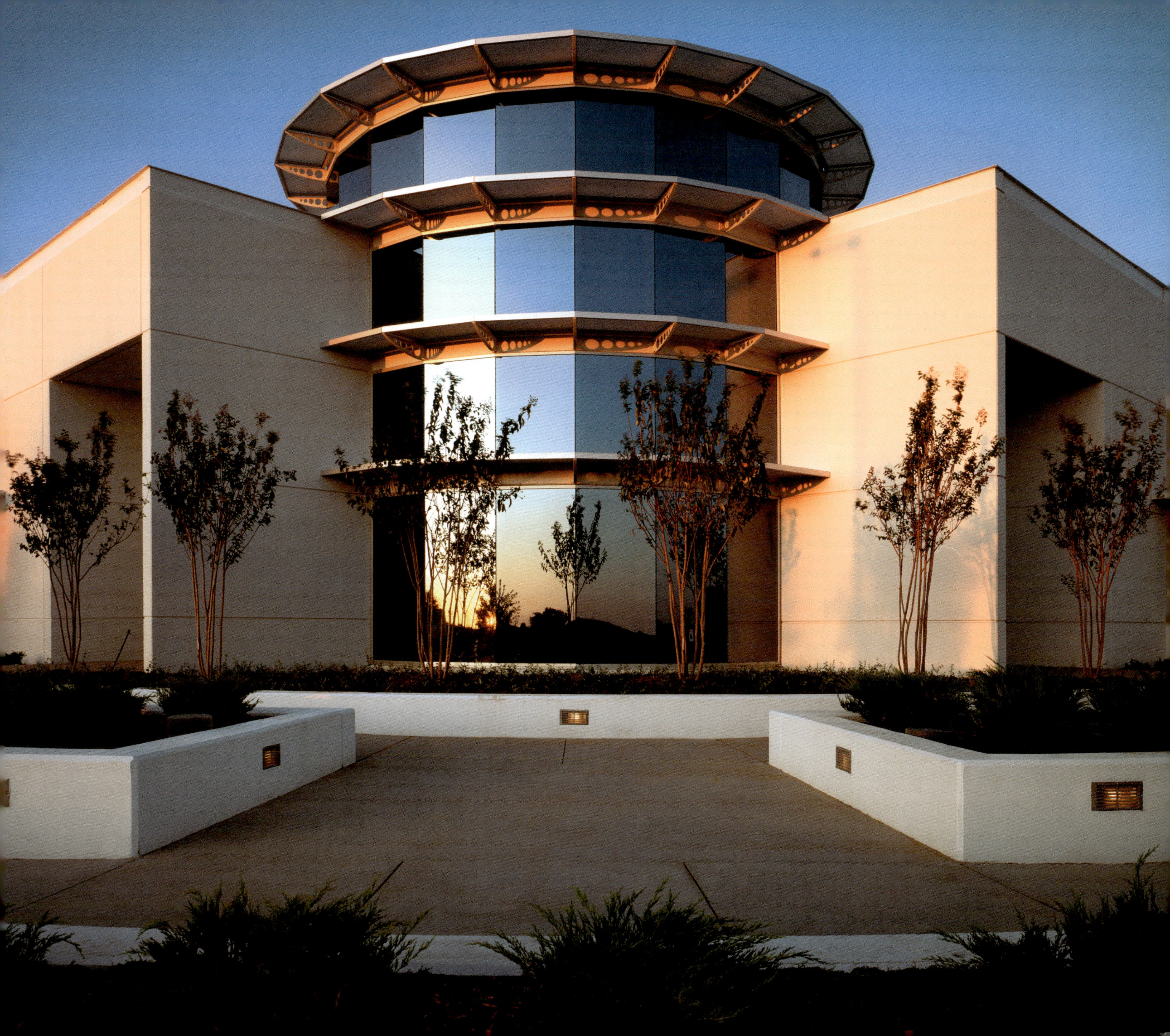

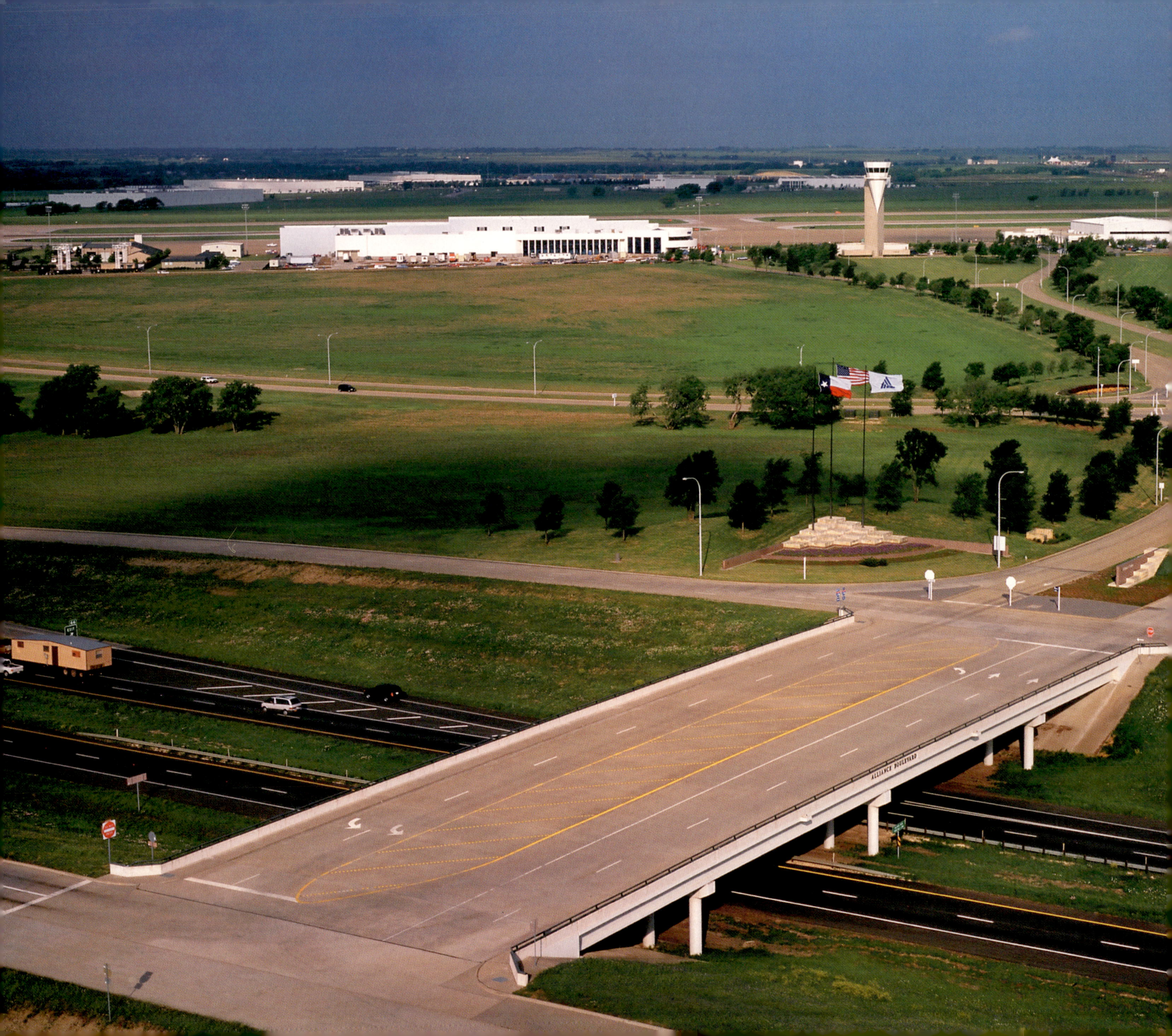
ALLIANCE BOULEVARD

Chapter Four A Unique Community

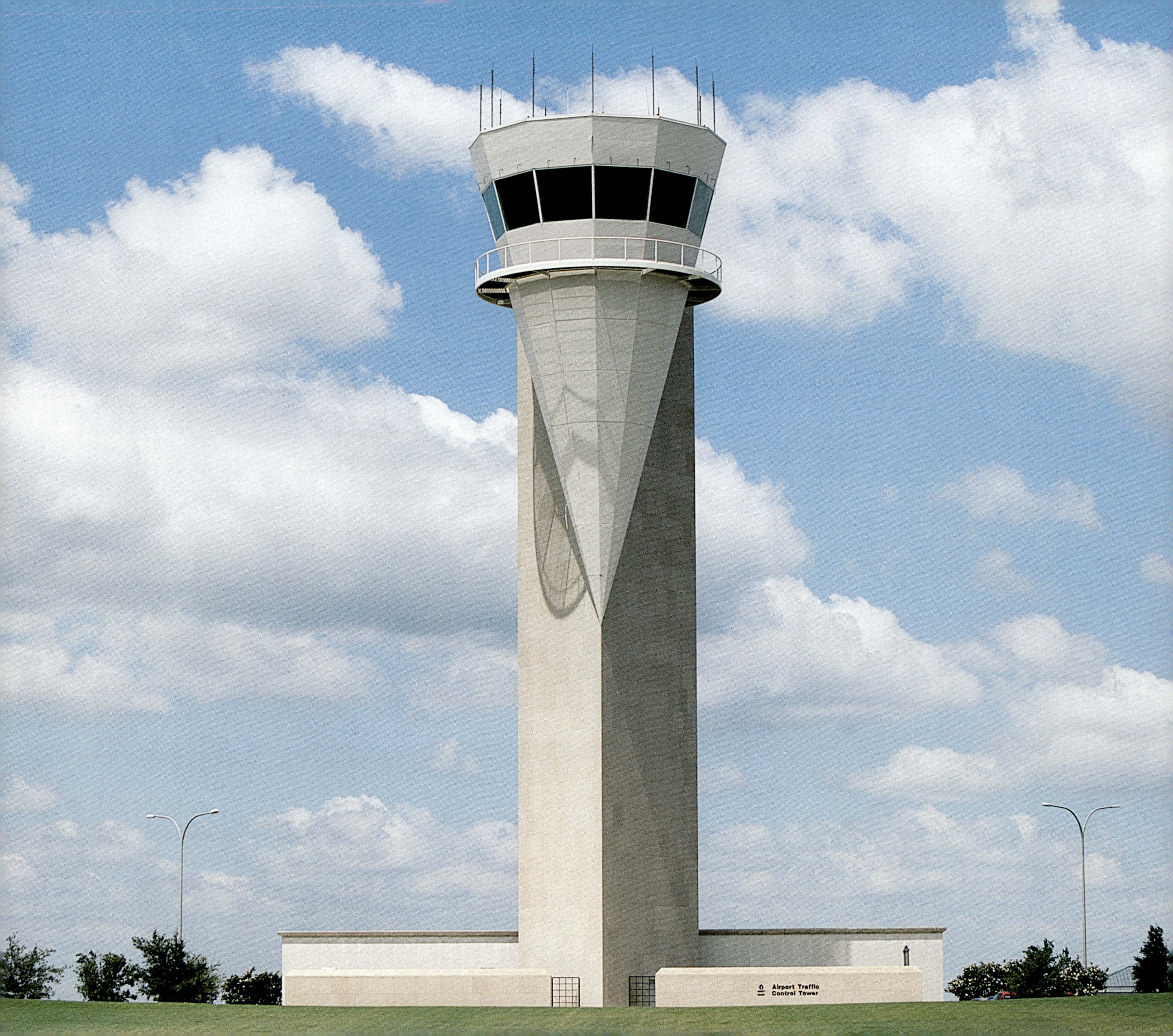
Airport Traffic
Control Tower

A UNIQUE COMMUNITY 45

As one examines the array of top companies that have chosen to locate facilities at Alliance, it is difficult to imagine a time when the community was just being pieced together. The first announcements had provided the development with credibility. However, the community still had only a few customers by the early 1990s.

The economic downturn had not yet lifted in Texas or in the nation. Few companies were expanding. Yet, the Alliance team was patiently making plans to ride the recovery when it came.

Perhaps, it was the lack of experience that proved to be one of the Alliance team's most valuable resources during these early building years. Looking back on this period, Hays Lindsley, one of Perot's first hires in 1986, jokes that the team was "unencumbered by experience."

"We didn't know any better. None of us had ever built an airport before," recalls Lindsley. "We didn't know it was supposed to be impossible." Accordingly, the team set out repeatedly with the goal of accomplishing the impossible.

The modern Alliance control tower, beside the former control tower, shines as a welcoming beacon to planes and visitors at night.

The Alliance control tower, completed in August of 1992, is a far cry from the early days when air traffic controllers had to operate out of a trailer.

CHAPTER FOUR

Planting Seeds

Marketing was the primary task for the Alliance team during the early 1990s. The team was tireless in its efforts and not afraid to attempt any strategy. Looking back on those years, Bill Burton, now a senior vice president and a member of the Alliance marketing team, describes the pace as "tough."

"We literally called anyone we could talk to," recalls Burton, who joined the project staff in 1990. "There were times when we would not even have a prospect list to take to our marketing meetings. We had a lot of imaginary deals back then."

Burton remembers calling on "hundreds" of companies simply searching for leads. He describes many of these calls as being "cold as cold could be." During these years, a critical tool was the *World Aviation Directory,* which lists executives from the aviation industry. Alliance marketing team members spent their days educating industry officials about the development.

Still, as the Alliance team engaged in the arduous task of informing the world about the development, occasional major announcements continued to reinforce their belief in the project. Among these were the 1993 decision by Federal Express to locate a sorting hub at Alliance and the 1994 decisions by Nokia Mobile Phones, Zenith Electronics and Riddell Athletic Footwear to establish facilities at the development.

Fred Smith, CEO of Federal Express, at the announcement of their regional sorting hub to be located at Alliance.

Right: In mid-1997, Federal Express, the world's largest express transportation company, opens a southwest regional automated hub at Alliance that can process 120,000 packages nightly. Located on 168 acres adjacent to the airport, the complex features seven buildings totaling 986,000 square feet, aircraft ramp areas and parking for delivery trucks. Fed Ex currently employs 975.

Above: An early construction shot of the Fed Ex sorting hub.
Left: The Fed Ex facility in operation.

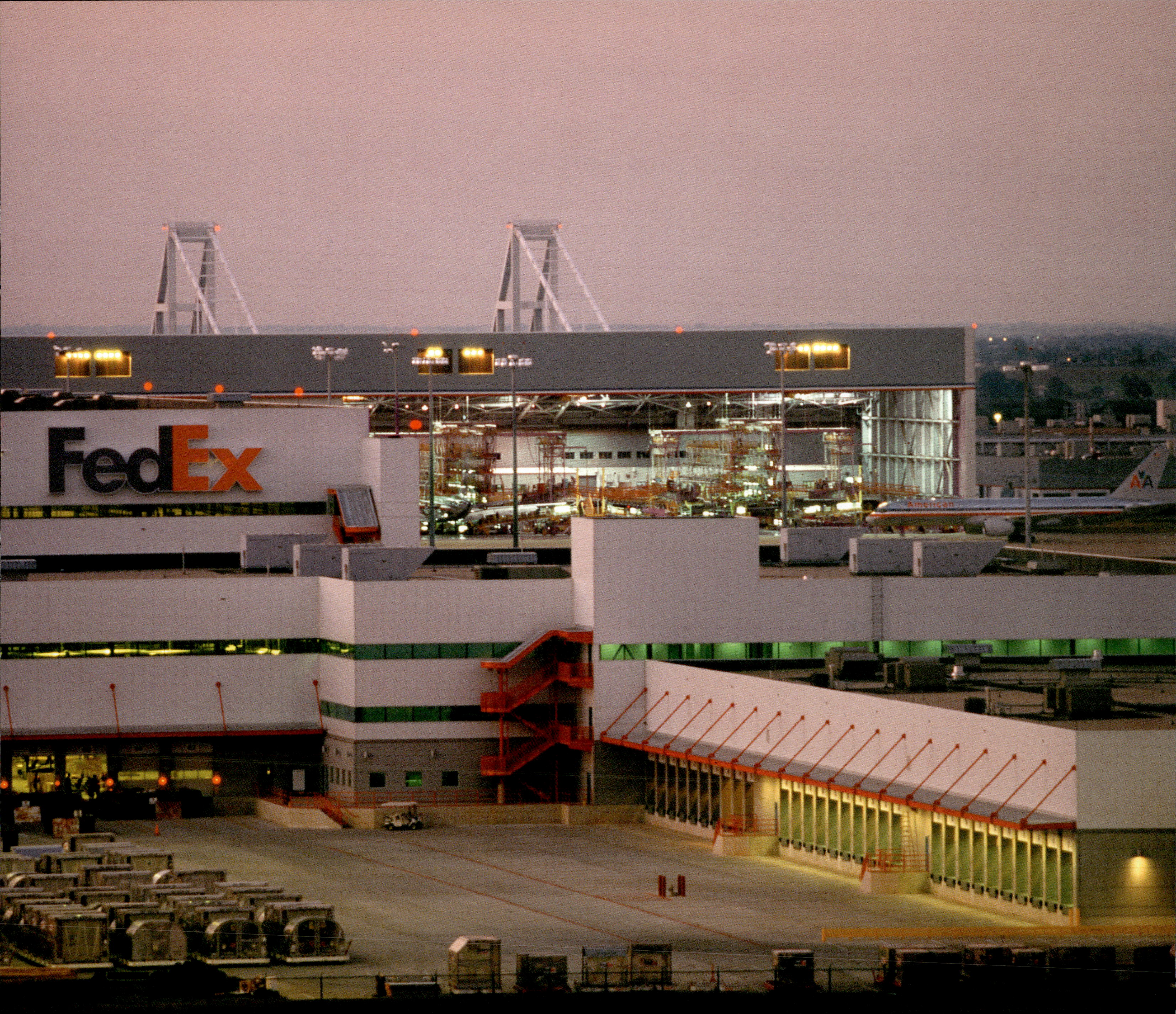
FedEx
American
AA

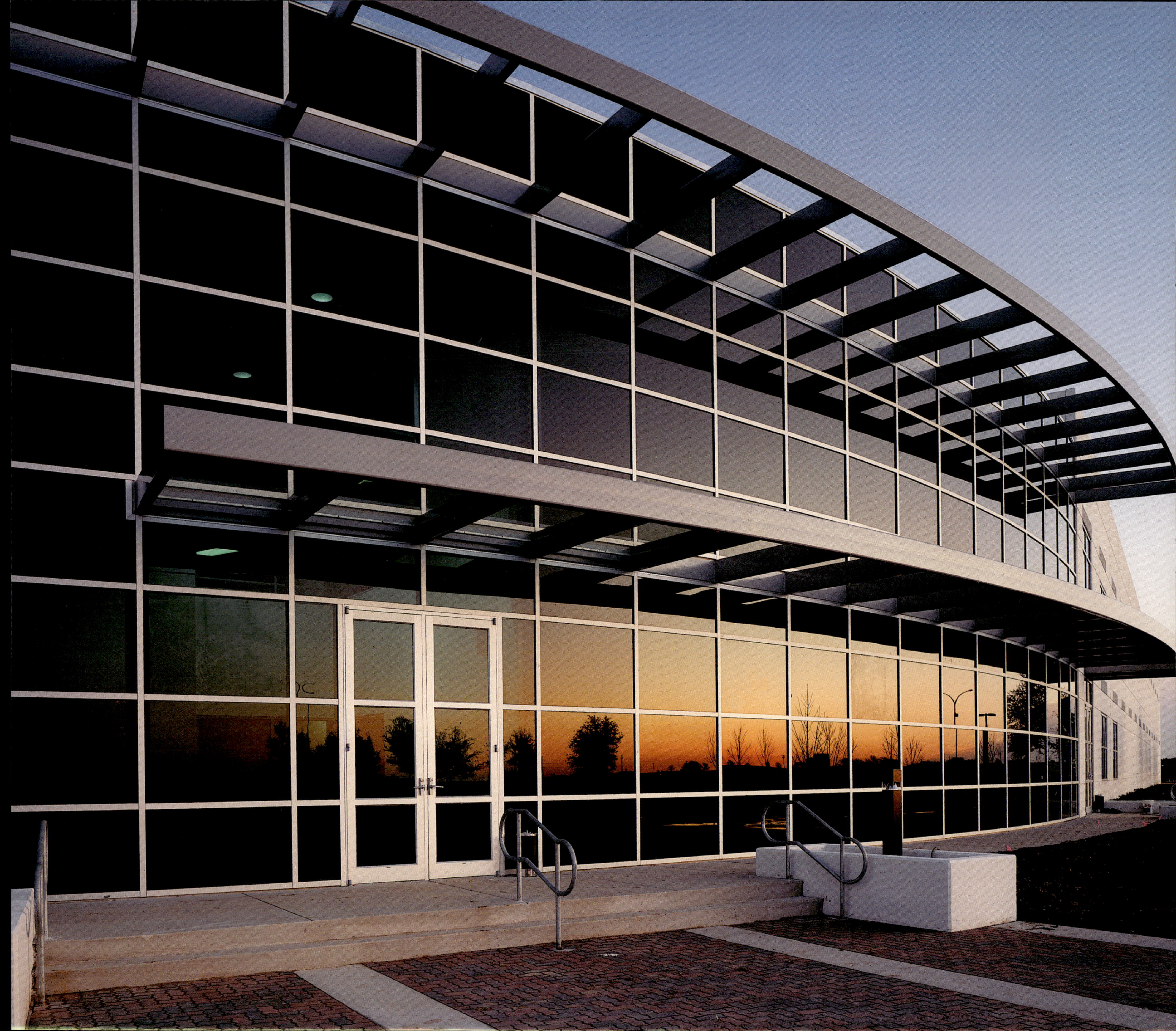

A UNIQUE COMMUNITY 49

Alliance Blooms

The seeds that had been planted during the early 1990s began to grow and blossom by the mid-1990s. That growth was prompted, in part, by the decision of Alliance team members to begin constructing warehouse space before orders were placed. These massive warehouses, built purely on speculation, allowed the development to offer immediate occupancy to prospective tenants. A period of rapid growth followed. As Burton puts it, "It was like someone flipped on a switch."

Since then, there has been a steady stream of announcements of new companies flocking to Alliance. The list of tenants is a virtual "Who's Who" of global businesses. Among the tenants are 22 Fortune 500 companies and more than 80 companies in total.

As the development has blossomed, the many players that helped to create Alliance have reaped great dividends. In addition to creating thousands of new jobs and generating tens of millions in new tax revenue, Alliance has become the No. 1 taxpayer in the cities of Fort Worth, Haslet and Roanoke and in the Northwest Independent School District. The development is also the third largest taxpayer in Tarrant County and the largest taxpayer in Denton County. Private companies have invested more than $3.8 billion in Alliance.

Alliance also led to the construction of Texas Motor Speedway on the development's northern edge. Hillwood sold the 950 acres on which the speedway sits to Bruton Smith in 1995. The speedway attracts more than 1 million visitors to the area each year. In addition, nationwide coverage of events held at the speedway allows millions more to see Alliance. Such exposure to the public is a critical ingredient in helping others to understand the vital role played by the development in terms of regional economic and job growth.

Left: Zenith, a leading manufacturer of consumer electronics and cable television products, uses a 499,797-square-foot warehouse and distribution building for its color television sets and videocassette recorders.

Right: The 2,400-acre Alliance Center attracts aviation-related companies such as Galaxy Aerospace and Federal Express, who enjoy direct taxiway access. This sector of Alliance also offers development sites for office, commercial and service-related companies.

Below: Employees of Alliance customers participate every year in the Corporate Challenge, an Olympic-style event.

Mitsubishi Motor Sales of America operates a 203,000-square-foot regional automotive parts distribution center on 14.4 acres in Alliance Gateway, employing 250.

Race car drivers, sponsors and race fans use the Alliance airport during NASCAR and Indy car races at Texas Motor Speedway.

Reaching Beyond Our Shores

The Alliance team has not stopped at this country's borders in its search for opportunity. Prospective customers from around the globe have been introduced to the Alliance development, as have U.S. exporters. Part of the attraction of Alliance for these global companies is the development's Foreign Trade Zone. With nearly 2,000 acres included in this area, Alliance represents one of the nation's largest foreign trade zones. The foreign trade zone at Alliance allows companies to import and export products and materials duty-free.

In addition to this foreign trade zone, Alliance is located in the North Fort Worth Enterprise Zone and is a member of the World Trade Centers Association.

These resources have combined to make Alliance a magnet for a wide array of businesses, including aviation companies, distribution operations, manufacturing facilities, cargo companies and others. Among the international companies that have located at Alliance are Nokia (Finland), Perlos (Finland), Recaro (Germany) and Nolato (Sweden). One of the partners in Galaxy Aerospace is Israel Aircraft Industries. The joint venture between the Italian firm Agusta and Bell Helicopter has located its headquarters at Alliance.

As Berry notes, Alliance has a "story" for almost any potential client. Accordingly, the best days for Alliance and all of those who benefit from the project may actually lie ahead.

Bell/Agusta Aerospace is set to open its headquarters and delivery center for the new 609 tilt-rotor aircraft at Alliance.

In June of 1999, Galaxy Aerospace opens its 160,897-square-foot world headquarters that includes an aircraft hangar for completion and maintenance activities, a parts distribution/logistics center, and customer support operations. The Astra SPX and Galaxy corporate jets are completed and serviced at the facility.

Above: In November of 1994, Nokia announces the expansion of its distribution center at Alliance.

Left: Left to right, Ross Perot Jr, chairman of Hillwood, Brian Barents, CEO of Galaxy Aerospace, and Kenneth Barr, mayor of Fort Worth, participate in the groundbreaking for the Galaxy Aerospace facility.

Right: In 1995, Finland-based Nokia, the world's leading mobile phone supplier, opens a manufacturing and distribution center and a service and repair center in the Alliance Gateway. In December of 1998, the Alliance facility produced its 100 millionth cell phone.

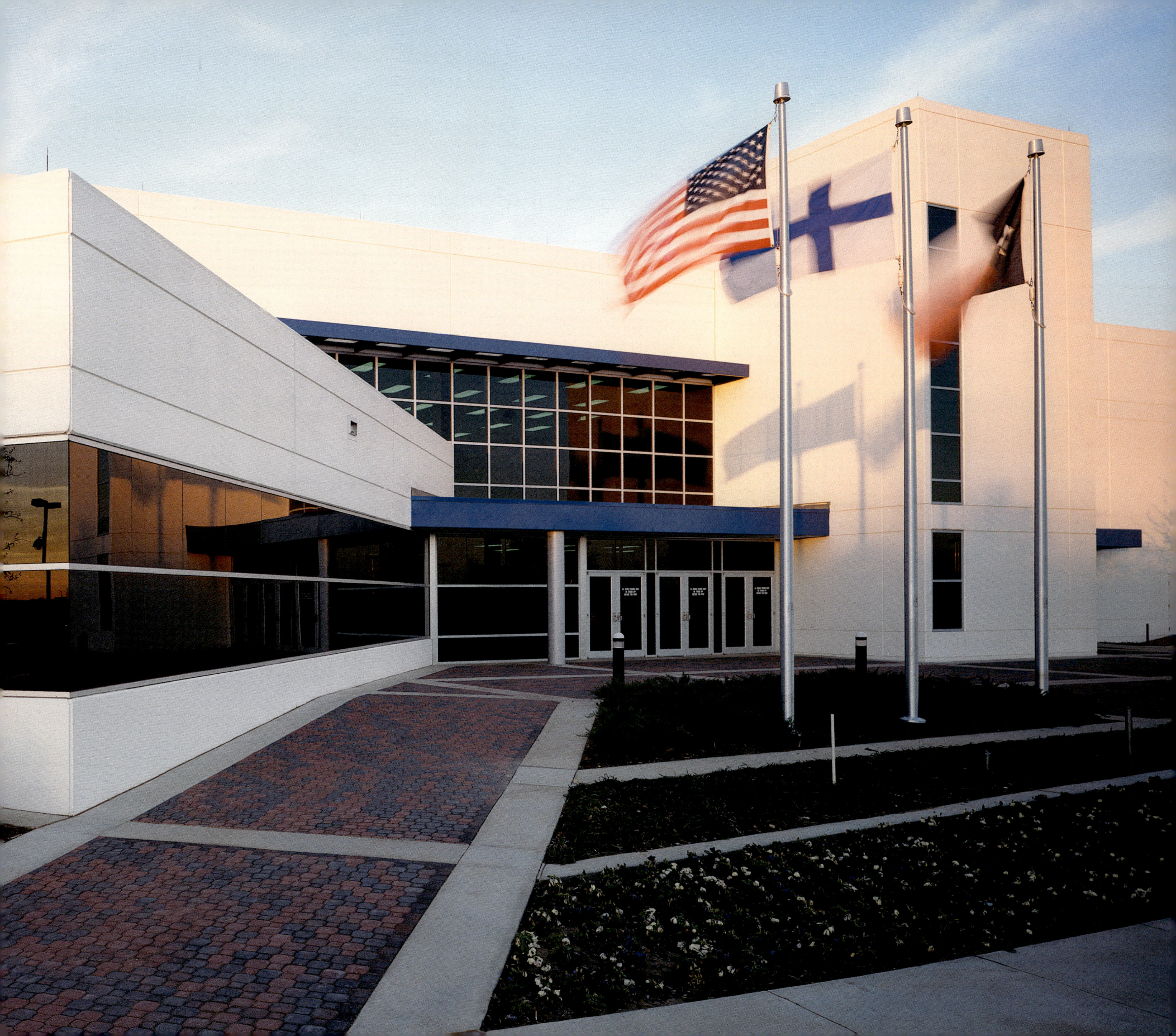

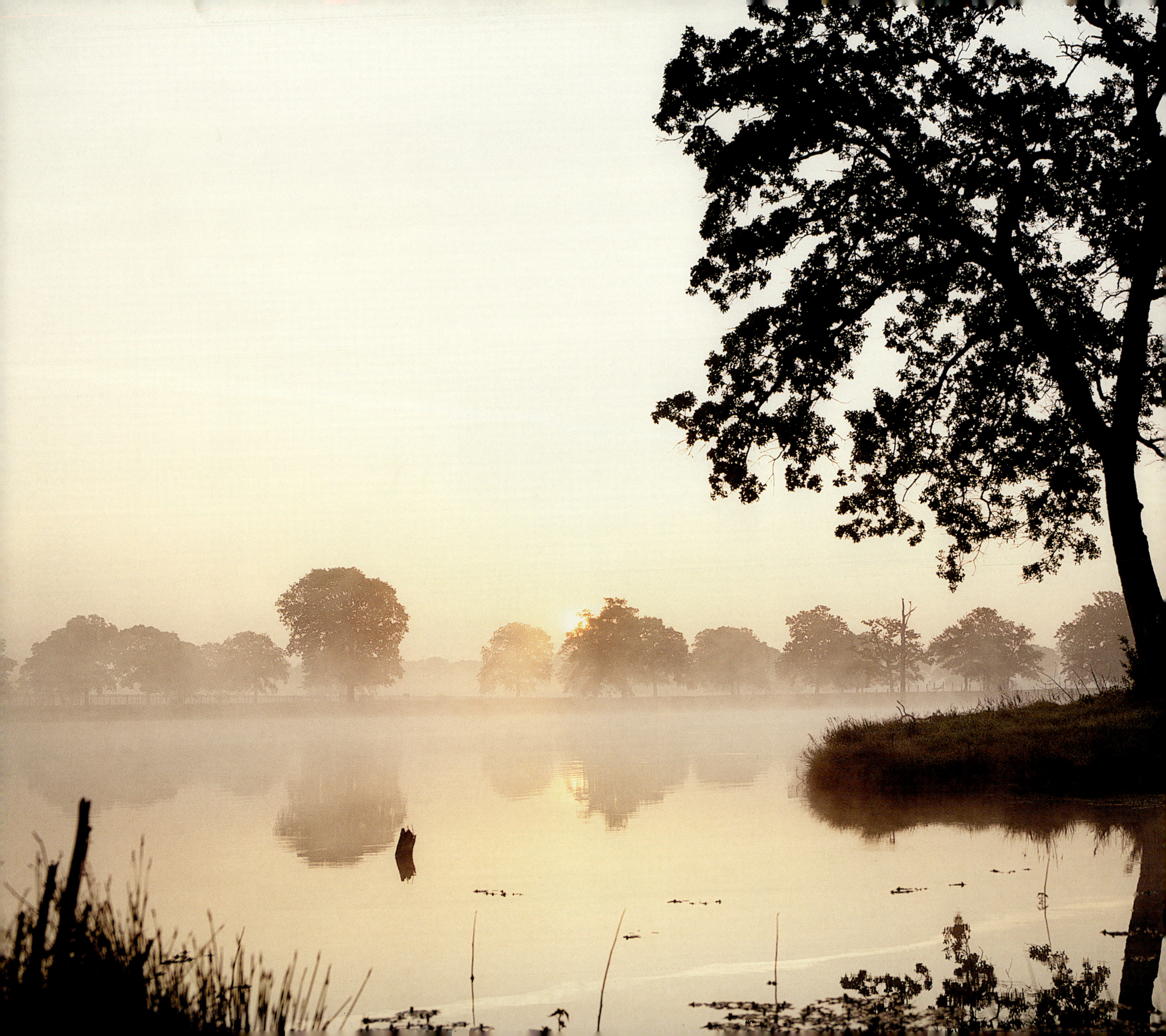

Chapter Five A Vision of the Future

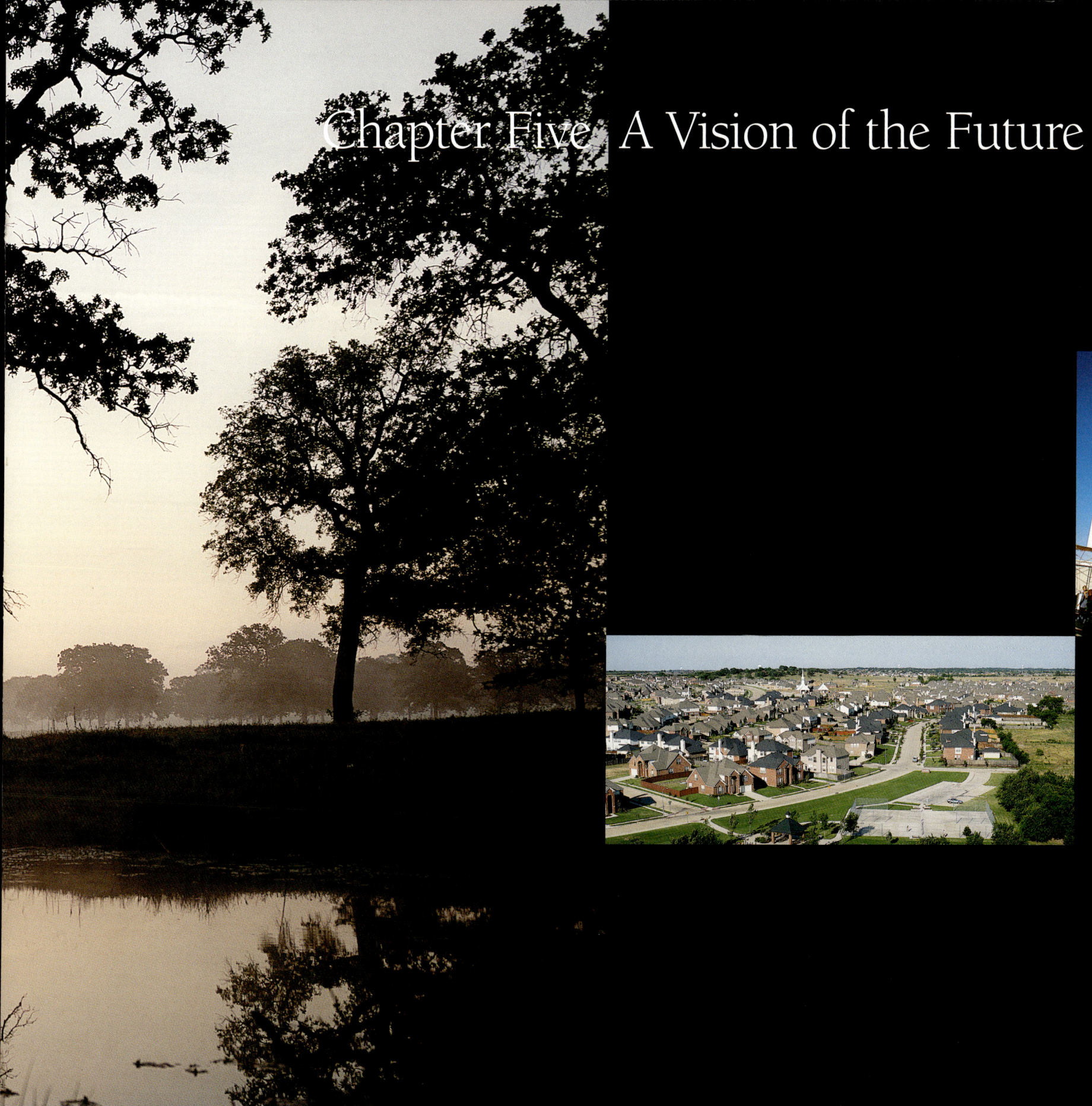

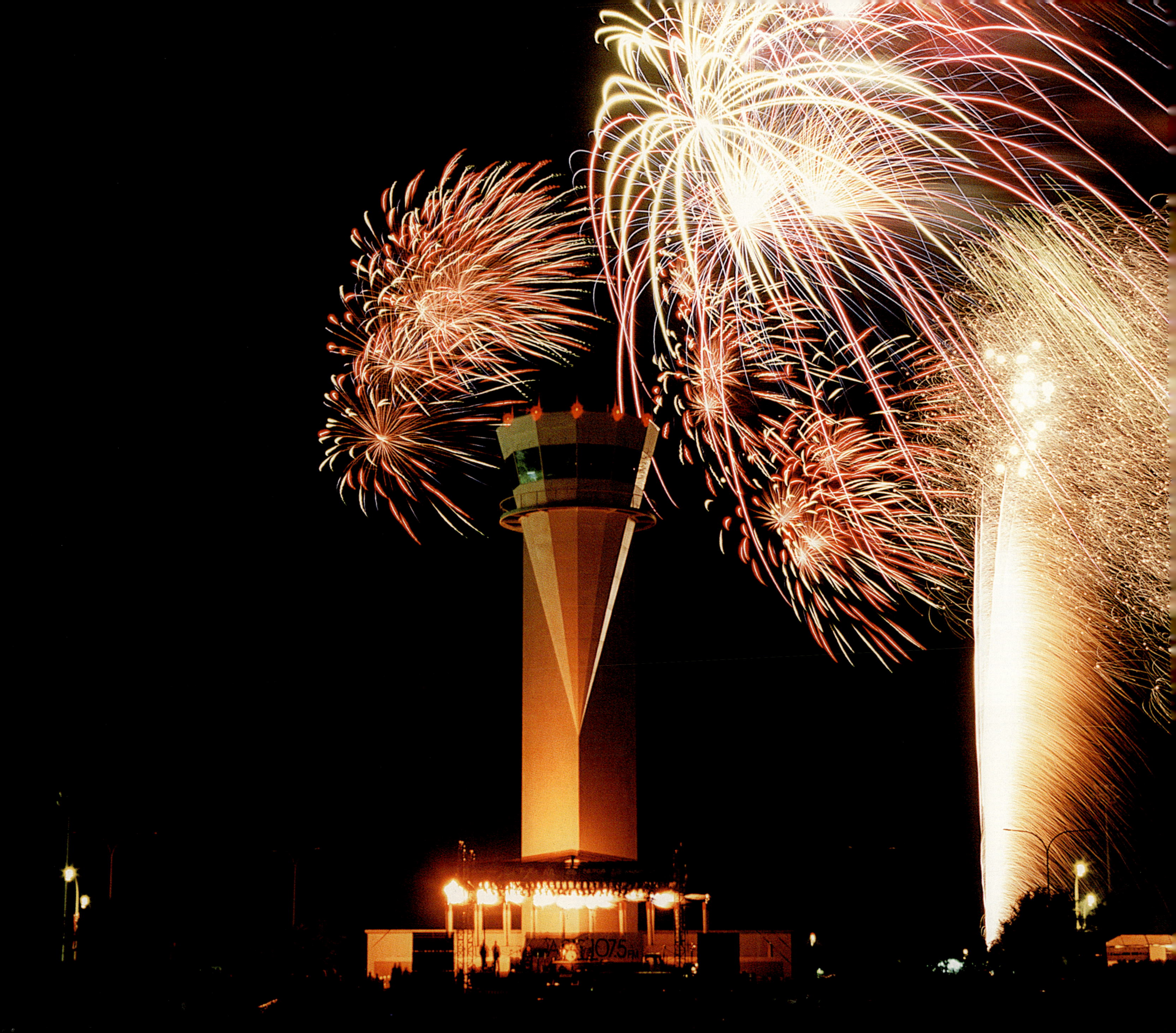
107.5

A VISION OF THE FUTURE 55

Alliance kick off its celebration of the 10th anniversary July 3, 1999, with a 10K run, a jazz concert with legendary performer Chuck Mangione, and a theatrical fireworks display.

Through the past decade, Alliance has helped to reshape the North Texas plains. Yet, despite the rapid growth of jobs and opportunity spurred by Alliance, the growth of the next decade may be far greater. With only 15 to 20 percent of the available land developed, Alliance has significant space for new tenants and future job growth.

In addition to Federal Express, Burlington Northern Santa Fe, Nokia and American Airlines, which have already located principal facilities at Alliance, and Intel, which is planning a major manufacturing center, Perot expects to see at least four more "anchor" tenants move into the Alliance community in coming years. The introduction of such facilities would likely produce thousands of new jobs. However, such expansion may be only the tip of the Alliance growth "iceberg."

The vision of "potential" helped turn Alliance from acres of raw land into a business entity without equal.

A Lifestyle

When Patterson speaks of future growth at Alliance, he considers the entire region. The Alliance corridor, he predicts, will become a "lifestyle." Accordingly, the headlines of the future may not be limited to industrial additions. Instead, he sees new retail facilities, entertainment opportunities, and residential options combining with the growth in the job market to attract new residents and strengthen the local community.

The presence of Alliance has allowed Hillwood to expand in the region and provide a wide variety of choices for industrial, office, residential and retail customers. Around the time that Alliance opened, Hillwood opened Park Glen, a 1,000-acre residential community that now houses more than 2,600 families.

Part of the reason for the growth in this area is the acquisition by Hillwood of the Circle T Ranch. The 2,500 acres that make up the famous ranch provide room for corporate campuses, golf courses, parks and retail space. As Patterson notes, the Circle T opens entirely new options for the development of the region.

In 1998, Hillwood began developing Circle T Ranch, just east of Alliance, and Heritage, just south of Alliance.

The picturesque rolling hills of the Circle T already have attracted a 314-acre corporate campus for Fidelity Investments, a 1.6 million-square-foot super regional shopping center, a resort hotel with a golf course designed by Pete Dye, a luxury residential community wrapped around a golf course planned by Tom Fazio, and a 35-acre hospital campus.

Although Circle T Ranch is a development that certainly could stand on its own, its roots stretch back to Alliance. "We would not

Located on the southern edge of Alliance along Interstate 35W, the 150-acre Alliance Crossing has a combination of retail and service establishments, including restaurants, banks, hotels and retail stores.

Hillwood team members compete in the plane pull, a part of the annual Alliance Corporate Challenge.

Park Glen is a master-planned residential community set on 1,000 acres south of Alliance. Designed for families, it includes a linear park with creek-lined picnic areas; soccer, football and baseball fields; playgrounds; tennis and basketball courts; greenbelts; and a hike-and-bike trail.

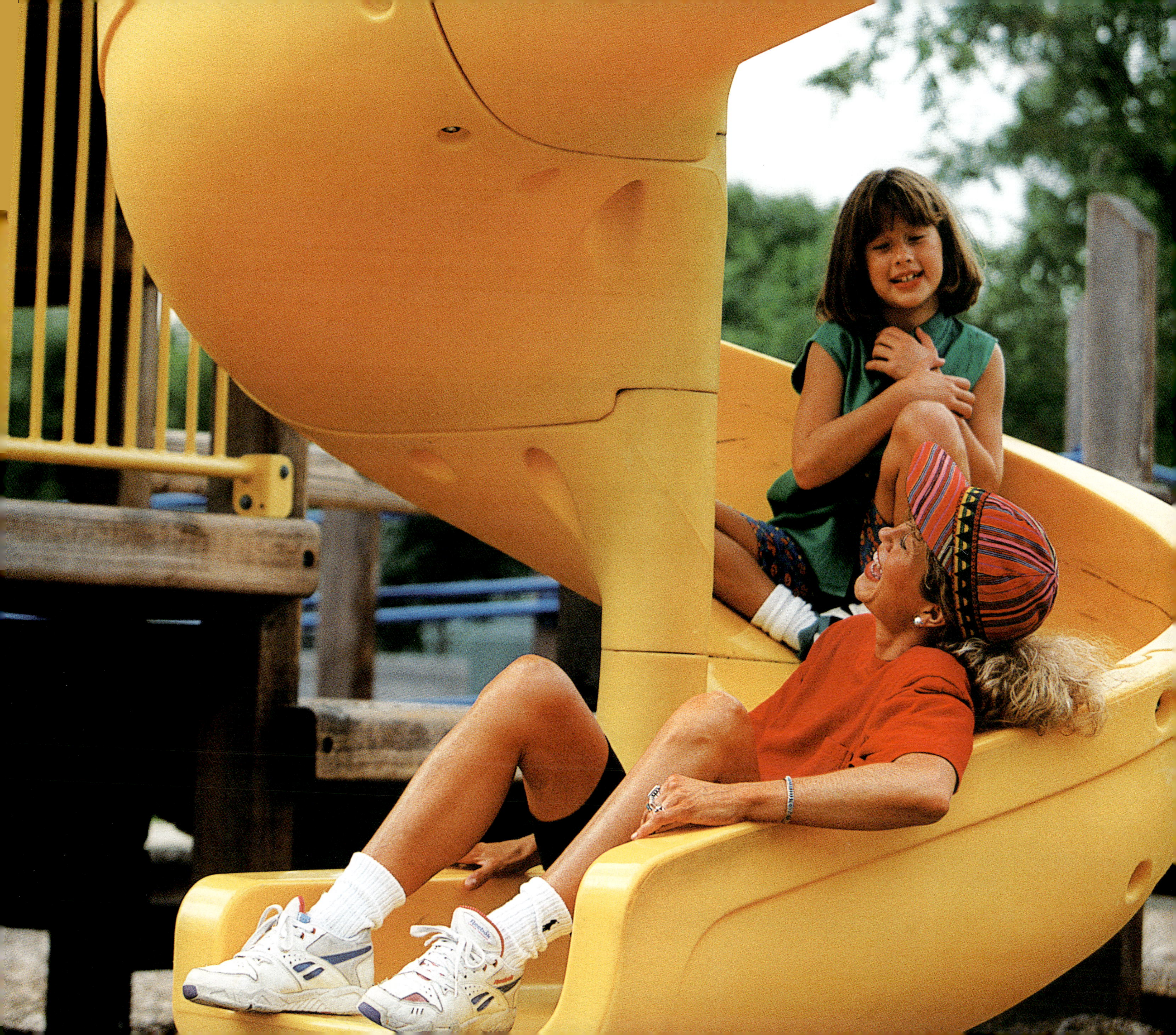

CHAPTER FIVE

The state-of-the-art JC Penney Distribution Center under construction.

Retail establishments have found a market in Alliance Crossing.

have purchased the Circle T if we did not already have the Alliance program," said Perot.

The 2,500-acre Heritage project is primarily a residential community that already includes a 54-acre master-planned park and an integrated school site program.

Berry also expects growth in high-technology companies moving into the area. The transportation facilities available at Alliance make it a prime location for a international e-commerce hub.

On the employment front, the Alliance team is estimating the number of jobs at the development to double during the next decade. Over the next 30 years, the number of jobs at Alliance could reach "50 to 60 thousand," according to Perot.

Of course, there are as many predictions about the direction of future growth at Alliance as there are existing tenants. However, one thing is certain. There is much of the Alliance story that is yet to be written. As Zaccanelli suggests, Alliance may be "just starting the second quarter," in terms of its growth. In fact, if his predictions are true, Alliance may still be growing decades into the future.

Perhaps, it is Perot, the mastermind behind the Alliance development who sums the future up best, by noting, "As long as Texas grows, we'll keep growing."

AREA RESIDENTS TAKE NOTICE

Alliance developers have worked to ensure that the project is more than an industrial facility. Today, the unusual blend of facilities at Alliance is attracting people from every walk of life.

Apart from the regular announcements of new corporate tenants, it is, perhaps, the annual airshows at Alliance that attract the greatest public attention. Each year since 1991, the facility has attracted military and civilian aircraft of every vintage and type. In addition, the events have included such top name acts as the Blue Angels flying team and the Thunderbirds. The shows have become a highlight for many in the local community, drawing 50,000 to 60,000 visitors per day, according to Tom Harris, Hillwood Properties senior vice president.

In addition to the annual airshows, a major focal point on the Alliance campus is the Texas Motor Speedway. This state-of-the-art sports and entertainment facility is the venue for NASCAR and Indy car races, as well as concerts and other events. With seating for more than 200,000, the facility is one of North Texas' major attractions.

In the future, the Alliance development is likely to offer even more opportunities for area residents. Among these may be educational facilities. Already, Texas Christian University has established satellite facilities at Alliance. These facilities are used to provide continuing education opportunities for corporate and area residents. Other universities are considering the establishment of similar facilities. According to Bolen, this can create a critical link between area universities, the Alliance development and the local community.

Other additions are also under consideration. As Harris notes, the Alliance team is willing to "take advantage of any opportunity to expand our vision."

59

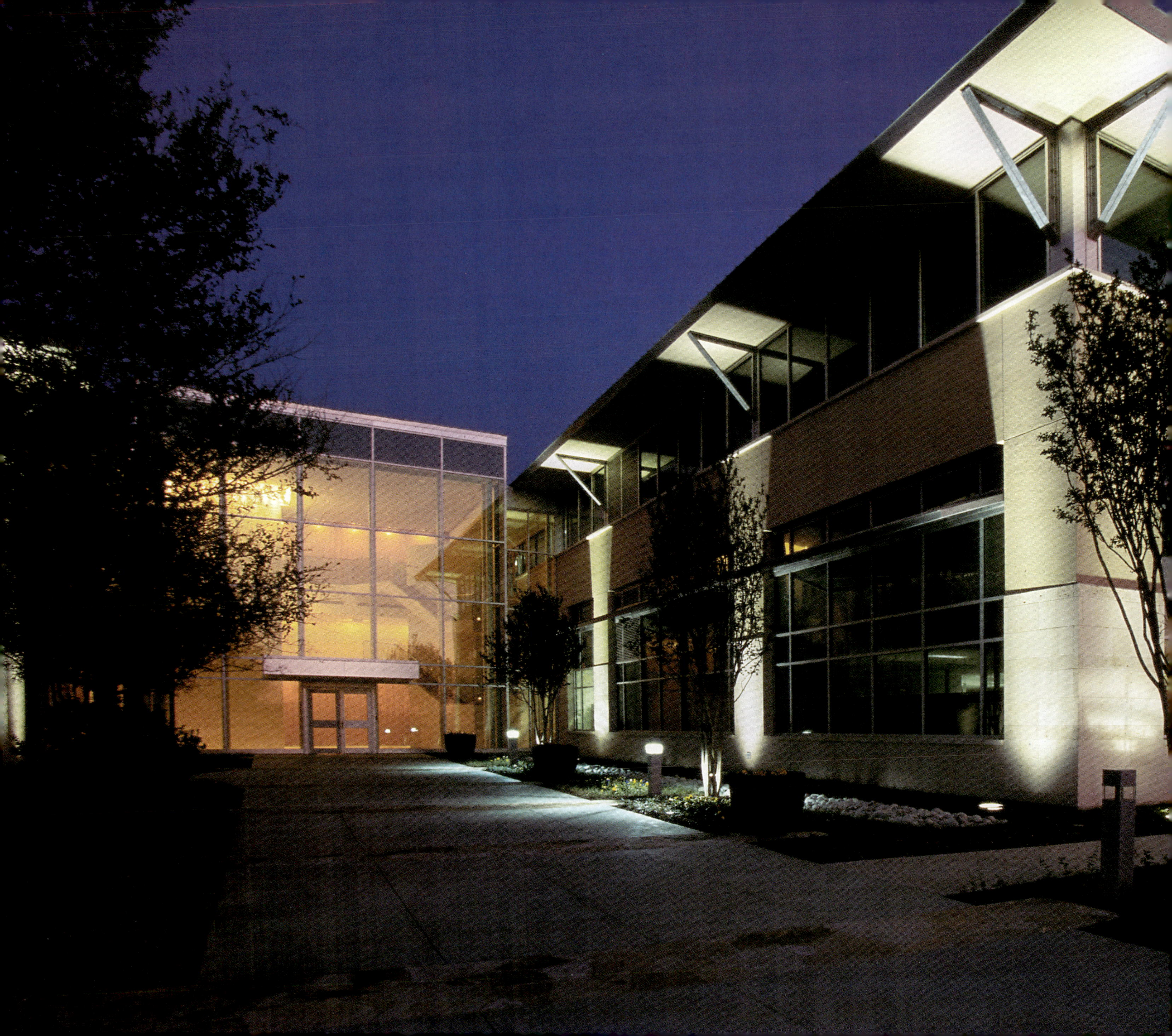

A Decade of Success

6 2   ALLIANCE

Larry Cain and Ross Perot Jr. at barbecue announcing plan for Alliance.

Frank Zaccanelli and former Haslet Mayor Bob Street.

Allan McArtor and wife Gracie.

Dub Blessing (longtime associate).

Pony Duke, Sharon Holman-Rae, and Iwo Nakatani, former representative of Ishida.

Tim Ward, Tom Harris, Alliance team members.

Robyn Kelly and Harry McKillop welcome Aeroflot to Alliance.

A Decade of Success

1988

JULY 9, 1988

- The official groundbreaking is held for **Fort Worth Alliance Airport**.

Ross Perot Jr. pointing to the first skid marks on the new Alliance runway.

American Airlines groundbreaking.

1989

MAY

- **Santa Fe Railway** becomes the first major customer at Alliance with its auto unloading facility.

JUNE

- **American Airlines** announces decision to locate its $482-million maintenance and engineering center at Alliance.

NOVEMBER

- The official groundbreaking is held for **American Airlines Maintenance and Engineering Center**.

DEC. 14, 1989

- **Fort Worth Alliance Airport** officially opens.

Santa Fe groundbreaking.

1990

JANUARY

- More than 1,000 acres are added at Alliance to accommodate future industrial users.

APRIL

- **Santa Fe Railway** expands Alliance auto distribution center for Ford and Honda.
- Construction begins on **Texas State Highway 170**.

JUNE

- Construction begins on Alliance Boulevard and Eagle Parkway.
- **Ishida Aerospace** announces plans to locate at Alliance.

SEPTEMBER

- **Food Lion** announces plans for a 1.3 million-square-foot distribution center in the Gateway section of Alliance.
- The **Federal Aviation Administration** moves from its temporary office to open a new Flight Standards District Office at Alliance.

A DECADE OF SUCCESS 63

Alliance team members: Isaac Manning, Mike Berry, Richard Squires, Tim McCabe, David Hardesty and Bill Burton.

Luncheon honoring Bob Street at Cactus Flower Café in 1993.

Tom Harris and Isaac Manning.

Darrell Lake and Bill Burton.

Mike Berry and Tim Ward.

1991

JANUARY
- The **U.S. Drug Enforcement Administration** selects Alliance for its Southwest Airwing headquarters.

OCTOBER
- The first **International Air Show** is held at Fort Worth Alliance Airport.

1992

MARCH
- Construction begins on the retail center at **Alliance Crossing** at the northwest corner of Interstate 35W and Westport Parkway.

MAY
- **Nestlé** announces a 520,00-square-foot regional distribution center in Alliance Gateway.

AUGUST
- The permanent **Air Traffic Control Tower** opens at the airport.

OCTOBER
- **MedAlliance** and **Cactus Flower Cafe** open in Alliance Crossing.

NOVEMBER
- **Santa Fe Railway** purchases an additional 124 acres to create one of the largest intermodal yards in the country in Westport at Alliance.

1993

MAY
- **Subway Restaurant** opens a sandwich shop in Alliance Crossing.
- **Patterson Dental Company** announces a new distribution center in the Alliance Commerce Center.

SEPTEMBER
- **Valmont Electric** announces a new national distribution and sales office.

OCTOBER
- Nearly 2,000 acres of Alliance are designated a foreign trade zone.
- A **U.S. Customs** office begins operations at the Fixed Base Operation at Fort Worth Alliance Airport.

NOVEMBER
- **FlightSafety International** opens a training academy.

DECEMBER
- **Federal Express** announces a new $300 million sorting hub.

Isaac Manning and Richard Squires (groundbreaking of Alliance Crossing).

Ed Freidrichs with Gensler, and Julian Beinart with MIT during Alliance Charette planning session with architects and team members.

Russell Laughlin and Johnie Daniel.

Richard Squires at Alliance Invitational Golf Tournament.

Karen Killman receiving Employee Recognition Award.

Alliance companies often participate in the Cowtown Brushup, a volunteer fall event.

Darcy Anderson at Alliance Air Show.

Chris Ash at Alliance Aviation Services.

A Decade of Success

John Korte at Alliance Aviation Services.

1994

FEBRUARY
- **Alliance Aviation Services**, which oversees Hillwood's full-service Fixed Based Operation, begins operations at the airport.

MAY
- **Republic Title** leases space in the Alliance Crossing retail center.

JULY
- **Riddell Athletic Footwear** announces a new national distribution center and corporate headquarters.

AUGUST
- **Zenith Electronics Corporation** announces a new 499,797-square-foot regional distribution center in the Gateway section of Alliance.
- **JRC International** announces a new R&D facility.

OCTOBER
- The official groundbreaking for the **Federal Express Southwest Regional Hub** is held.

NOVEMBER
- **Nokia, Inc.** announces a new 424,000-square-foot manufacturing facility and distribution center in Alliance Gateway, creating 2,000 new jobs.
- **Trans-Trade, Inc.** leases 727 square feet in the retail center.

1995

JANUARY
- **CompuCom Systems, Inc.** opens a new warehouse and distribution center in Alliance Commerce Center.

MARCH
- **Personnel Connection, Inc.** (now Westaff) opens a temporary and full-time staffing agency in Alliance Crossing.

MAY
- **Perlos, Inc.**, a plastic components supplier to Nokia, leases space in the Alliance Commerce Center.

DECEMBER
- **PC Service Source**, a distributor of computer parts, opens a national distribution facility.
- **Marriott Distribution Services** opens a 127,200-square-foot food-service distribution center in the Westport section at Alliance.

A DECADE OF SUCCESS 65

Russell Laughlin and Larry Cain.

Kathy and Herb Middleton have handled security duties at Alliance for many years.

Ross Perot Jr. with Jack Sasser, FAA administrator.

On June 23, 1997, the Alliance Community of Companies presented Northwest Independent School District with a check for winning the "Alliance for Excellence in Education" award.

Rick Patterson and Mike Berry at Alliance Invitational Golf Tournament.

1996

JANUARY
- **Wendy's** and **Mobil** open in the convenience center at Alliance Crossing.

MARCH
- **James River Paper Company** (now Fort James) announces a 375,000-square-foot distribution center in the Gateway.
- **Eli Lilly** announces a national mail-order pharmacy center for its subsidiary PCS Health Systems. (PCS Health Systems has since been purchased by Rite Aid.)
- **Tech Data**, a computer parts and software company, announces a 250,000-square-foot distribution facility.
- **Dr. Misra, D.D.S.** signs a lease for the first dental office at Alliance.

APRIL
- The Alliance Commerce Center 4 building opens with **BF Goodrich Aerospace**, now Unison Industries, as lead tenant.

MAY
- **Marconi Instruments, Inc.** selects Alliance for worldwide operations and headquarters.
- **Comp USA** announces a 66,433-square-foot computer configuration and distribution center.
- **Michaels Stores** opens a 407,000 square foot regional distribution facility in the Westport section of Alliance.
- **Kinder Temporary Services, Inc.** signs a lease for 974 square feet in Alliance Crossing.

JUNE
- **Westport Physical Therapy and Rehabilitation Center** signs a lease for 2,922 square feet in the retail center.
- **Bank One** signs a lease to operate an Automated Teller Machine within the convenience center.
- **Mitsubishi Motor Sales of America** announces a 203,000-square-foot regional parts distribution facility in the Gateway.
- **Maytag** opens a 237,000-square-foot southwestern distribution center in the Westport section of Alliance.
- **Joe's Pizza** leases space in the convenience center at Alliance Crossing.

AUGUST
- **Texas Instruments** selects Alliance Gateway for its 409,914-square-foot North American distribution center.

SEPTEMBER
- **Applied Industrial Technologies** announces a 127,000-square-foot manufacturing and distribution center in the Gateway.

OCTOBER
- **JCPenney** announces a new 1.2 million-square-foot, state-of-the-art distribution center in the Westport section of Alliance.
- **Sonny Bryan's Smokehouse** signs a lease for a barbecue restaurant in the retail center.

NOVEMBER
- **Intel** announces a $1.3 billion, 800,000-square-foot advanced logic computer chip manufacturing plant to be based in the Advanced Technology Center.

Ribbon cutting for BF Goodrich Aerospace

Children of Alliance team members enjoy the annual Alliance Airshow.

Rick Patterson, Bill Burton and Calvin Peterson.

Ted Hinchman, Art Hammonds and Jay Hayes at Employee Awards presentation celebrating the Intel land sale.

Kim Thigpen, Mary Jane Ashmore, Cathy Black, Judy Franco (sitting) at party after Galaxy groundbreaking.

Corporate Challenge contestant "tastes" victory.

Alliance Challenge team members from 1997.

A Decade of Success

JC Penney groundbreaking.

Intel groundbreaking

1997

FEBRUARY
- **Kraft Foods** announces a new Southwest distribution campus, featuring a 400,000 square-foot dry goods distribution center and a 250,000-square-foot refrigerated products distribution center in the Westport section of Alliance.

APRIL
- **Hampton Inn & Suites** becomes the first hotel to locate at Alliance with a 95-room property.
- **SC Johnson Wax** chooses Alliance for a 192,000-square-foot regional distribution center in the Westport section of Alliance.
- **Bell Helicopter Textron** signs lease for an office at Fort Worth Alliance Airport.

MAY
- **Images Repographics** opens a retail outlet in the convenience center.
- **Southwestern Bell Telephone** announces a 215,062-square-foot corporate call center in the Gateway.
- **Southwest Freight** leases space for trucking and container dispatching in Alliance Commerce Center.

JUNE
- **General Mills** leases 367,815 square feet for a distribution center in the Westport section of Alliance.

JULY
- The official groundbreaking for the **JCPenney Distribution Center** in Westport at Alliance is held.
- **Intel** holds the official groundbreaking for its computer chip manufacturing plant.
- **International Aviation Composites** announces a new corporate headquarters and aviation service facility at Alliance.

AUGUST
- **Galaxy Aerospace** announces development of a new 160,897-square-foot, state-of-the-art hangar and headquarters at Alliance.
- **MagneTek** announces a new national distribution center in the Gateway.
- **Tucker Rocky Distributing** announces a 177,632-square-foot corporate headquarters and distribution center in Alliance Gateway.

DECEMBER
- **Hawthorn Suites** announces development of a hotel at Alliance Crossing.

1998

JANUARY
- **Air Alaska** selects 1,980 square feet for office space in Alliance Center.
- The 54,475-square-foot **Heritage Commons** opens as the first office facility at Alliance.

FEBRUARY
- **Sunstate Equipment Company** announces a new 8,000-square-foot branch office in Westport at Alliance.
- **DDH Aviation, Inc.** signs a lease for an office at Fort Worth Alliance Airport.

MARCH
- **Perlos, Inc.** expands operations and doubles space by relocating to an 81,693-square-foot facility in Alliance Gateway.
- **Beverage Canners International** leases 182,423 square feet for a new state-of-the-art water bottling and distribution facility in Alliance Gateway.

Hillwood team members gather for a group photo at the open house celebrating the opening of Heritage Commons.

A DECADE OF SUCCESS   67

Jo Peña, Marie Crump, Kim Thigpen, Mary Jane Ashmore, Franetta Savage, Jennifer Richardson and Shirley Williams.

Jack Morris.

Sharla Huddleston and Franetta Savage.

Bill Burton, Bob Bolen and Mike Berry.

Kim Thigpen, Lori Ticknor, Shirley Williams and Margaret Fox.

Corporate Challenge sponsors.

APRIL
- **HighTech FotoSign** leases 1,174 square feet for a retail outlet in Alliance Crossing.
- The **Fort Worth Police Department** opens a police substation in the retail center at Alliance Crossing.

MAY
- **Alliance Opportunity Center** opens an office dedicated to finding and training employees for Alliance-area businesses.
- **AT&T** leases a 221,000-square-foot facility in the Gateway for a cellular phone fulfillment center.

JUNE
- The 850-acre expansion of **Alliance Gateway** is completed with the final acquisition of 180 acres.

Alliance Opportunity Center opening.

AUGUST
- **W.W. Grainger** leases a 160,153-square-foot distribution facility for industrial and commercial equipment and supplies in Westport at Alliance.
- **Pro-Cuts** signs a lease for an 879-square-foot hair salon in Alliance Crossing.

OCTOBER
- The Urban Land Institute presents Alliance with the **ULI Award for Excellence** in the business park, large-scale category.
- **DSC Logistics** becomes the first resident in the 850-acre expansion of Alliance Gateway with the purchase of 30 acres to build a 600,000-square-foot distribution center.
- Hillwood and Longistics form **Alliance Operating Services**, a joint venture to provide third-party logistics services, including working in the Alliance foreign trade zone.
- **Manpower**, a personnel staffing agency, signs a lease for a 1,523-square-foot branch office in Alliance Crossing.

NOVEMBER
- **Oriental Garden** signs a lease for a 4,145-square-foot Chinese buffet restaurant in Alliance Crossing.
- **HeliFlite Shares**, an innovator in corporate helicopter fractional ownership, leases space for an office in Alliance Crossing.

DECEMBER
- **Nolato Texas** leases 39,884 square feet in the Alliance Commerce Center for a manufacturing center.
- **The Dallas Business Journal** signs a lease for a 974-square-foot bureau in Alliance Crossing.

Alliance Gateway

The Spirit of Enterprise Award is presented to Alliance Development Corporation.

Gidge Reed and Shirley Williams during ground control run.

Hillwood team participates in "Khakis for Kids," a fund-raiser for children.

Mary Jane Ashmore with Uncle Sam at jazz and fireworks festival.

Hillwood employees participate in 5K run.

Bill Walker and Calvin Peterson at Valeo groundbreaking.

M of D walkathon participants in April of 1999.

A Decade of Success

1999

JANUARY

- **Randalls Food Markets** signs the largest lease in Alliance history, 976,471 square feet in Alliance Gateway.
- **Norwest Bank** signs a lease for 3,706 square feet to open a banking center in Alliance Crossing.

MARCH

- **Ameritrade** announces a call center and customer service site, totaling 187,644 square feet in Alliance Gateway.
- **John Deere** leases 287,240 square feet for its regional distribution center for its consumer products in Alliance Gateway.
- **Nokia** expands into the 74,000-square-foot Gateway 15 building, giving the company 498,000 square feet at Alliance.
- **Tech Data** expands its existing 254,000-square-foot distribution facility by 285,000 square feet.
- The **United States Post Office** announces a 5,809-square-foot, full-service retail outlet in Alliance Crossing.
- **Schlotzsky's** opens a sandwich shop at Alliance Crossing.
- **Remedy Staffing** leases approximately 2,800 square feet in Alliance Crossing.

APRIL

- **Recaro Aircraft Seating** leases 61,088 square feet in the Alliance Commerce Center for its first U.S. assembly hub.
- **Perlos** leases an additional 98,000 square feet to be built on to their existing 82,000-square-foot facility in Alliance Gateway.
- **Taco Bueno** announces the development of a restaurant in Alliance Crossing.
- **Jet City, Inc.** signs a lease for 502 square feet in the airport hangar.

JUNE

- **Children's Courtyard** announces the development of a 13,600-square-foot day care center to serve approximately 190 children.
- **Triple S Plastics** leases 60,000 square feet for a manufacturing facility in Alliance Commerce Center.

JULY

- **Bell/Agusta Aerospace Company** announces the development of its new 16-acre headquarters at Alliance Center as a tilt-rotor training and delivery center.

AUGUST

- **Hewlett-Packard** leases 192,177 square feet in Alliance Gateway for a national distribution center.

SEPTEMBER

- **Texas Christian University** leases 15,784 square feet in Alliance Center for its TCUGlobalcenter.
- **Valeo Electronics** announces the purchase of 7 acres in the Alliance Advanced Technology Center for a 65,000-square-foot manufacturing facility.

OCTOBER

- **Savcor Coatings**, a supplier to Nokia, announces the lease of 42,025 square feet for a manufacturing and distribution facility in Alliance Commerce Center.

Raising the Alliance 10 year anniversary flag.

General Steve Ritchie at the 1999 Alliance Airshow.

Chuck Mangione performs at the Jazz and Lights in the Night Festival as part of Alliance's 10 year anniversary celebration.

A Decade of Progress

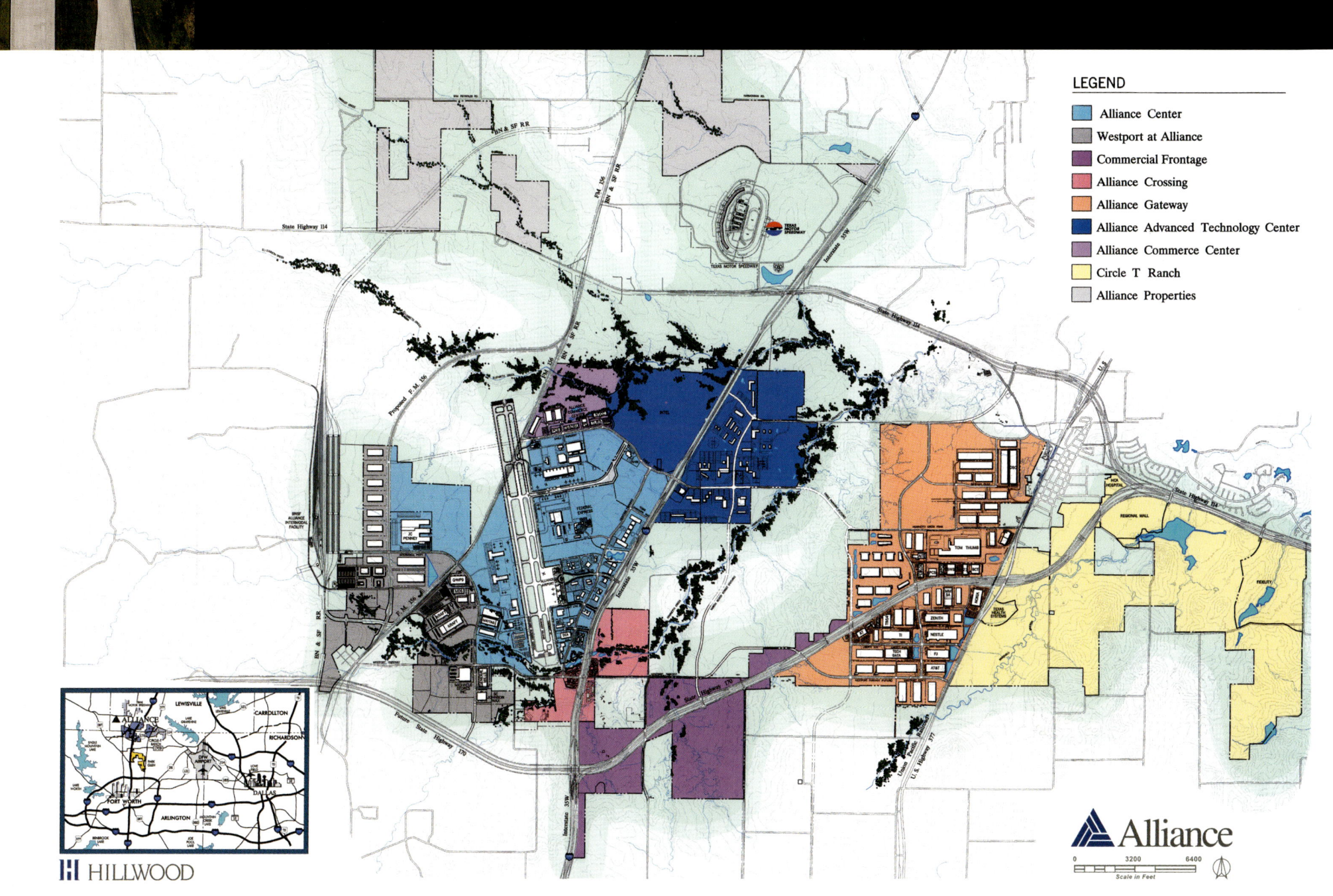

LEGEND

- Alliance Center
- Westport at Alliance
- Commercial Frontage
- Alliance Crossing
- Alliance Gateway
- Alliance Advanced Technology Center
- Alliance Commerce Center
- Circle T Ranch
- Alliance Properties

HILLWOOD

Alliance

February 1992 *April 1996* *May 1997*

Alliance Gateway

One of the busiest sectors at Alliance, the 2,350-acre Alliance Gateway is home to both distribution and manufacturing companies who can choose to build or lease warehouse-style facilities. Located on the eastern border of the project, the Gateway offers corporate residents one of the most sophisticated transportation networks in the country.

Rail access is provided by the Union Pacific Railway's main north-south transcontinental line on the eastern side. State Highway 170, a 6.8-mile freeway built to help connect Alliance to DFW International Airport, assists businesses further with their distribution needs. Also, a network of interchanges provides easy access to other nearby transportation facilities, including Burlington Northern Santa Fe's intermodal complex, Alliance Airport, and numerous major freeway arteries.

Residents of the Gateway include Randalls Food Markets, Nestlé, Nokia, Zenith Electronics Corporation, PC Service Source, Texas Instruments, Tech Data, AT&T, Mitsubishi Motor Sales of America, Fort James, Applied Industrial Technologies, Southwestern Bell Telephone, Tucker Rocky Distributing, MagneTek, Perlos, Beverage Canners International, DSC Logistics, John Deere, Hewlett-Packard, Children's Courtyard and Ameritrade.

January 1999

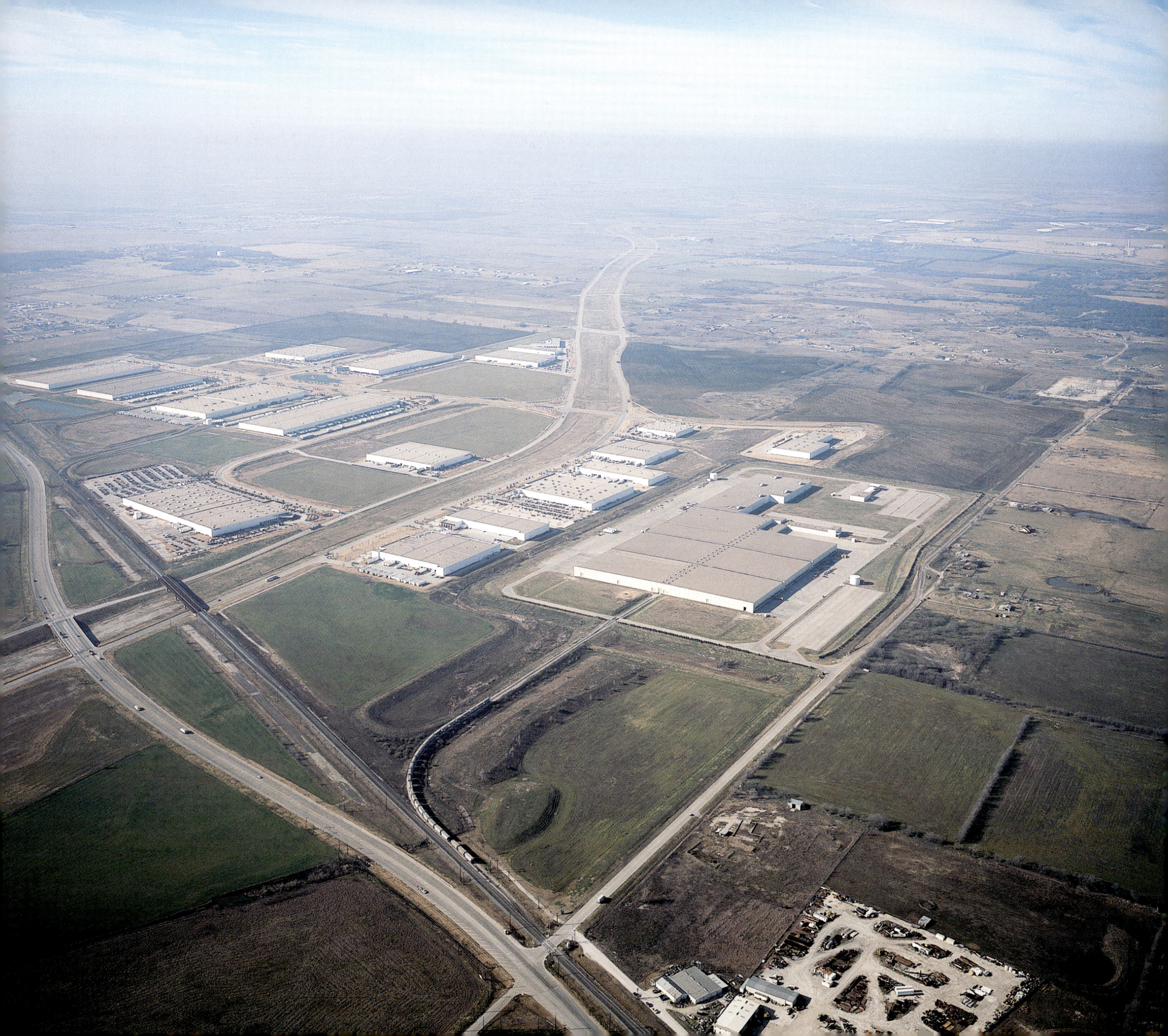

September 1992 *October 1995* *June 1997*

Westport at Alliance

The sprawling, 1,200-acre Westport at Alliance is designed for companies requiring immediate rail access, as well as other multimodal transportation solutions. Located adjacent to Burlington Northern Santa Fe's main north-south transcontinental rail line on the west side of Alliance, the sector is anchored by the rail company's 735-acre, $115 million state-of-the-art intermodal yard and 55-acre carload transportation center. The railroad encompasses 42 miles of new rail track and eight miles of relocated main-line track. This direct rail access offers corporate residents at Alliance connections to markets throughout the United States, Mexico and Canada.

Many companies take advantage of the sophisticated rail complex that offers a type of transportation that is both economical and efficient. Intermodal shipping involves moving freight by more than one method of transportation. Internationally known businesses such as BNSF, Marriott Distribution Services, Maytag, Michael's Stores, SC Johnson Wax, JCPenney, Kraft Foods, General Mills, International Aviation Composites, Sunstate Equipment Company and W.W. Grainger have located their facilities in this sector.

April 1999

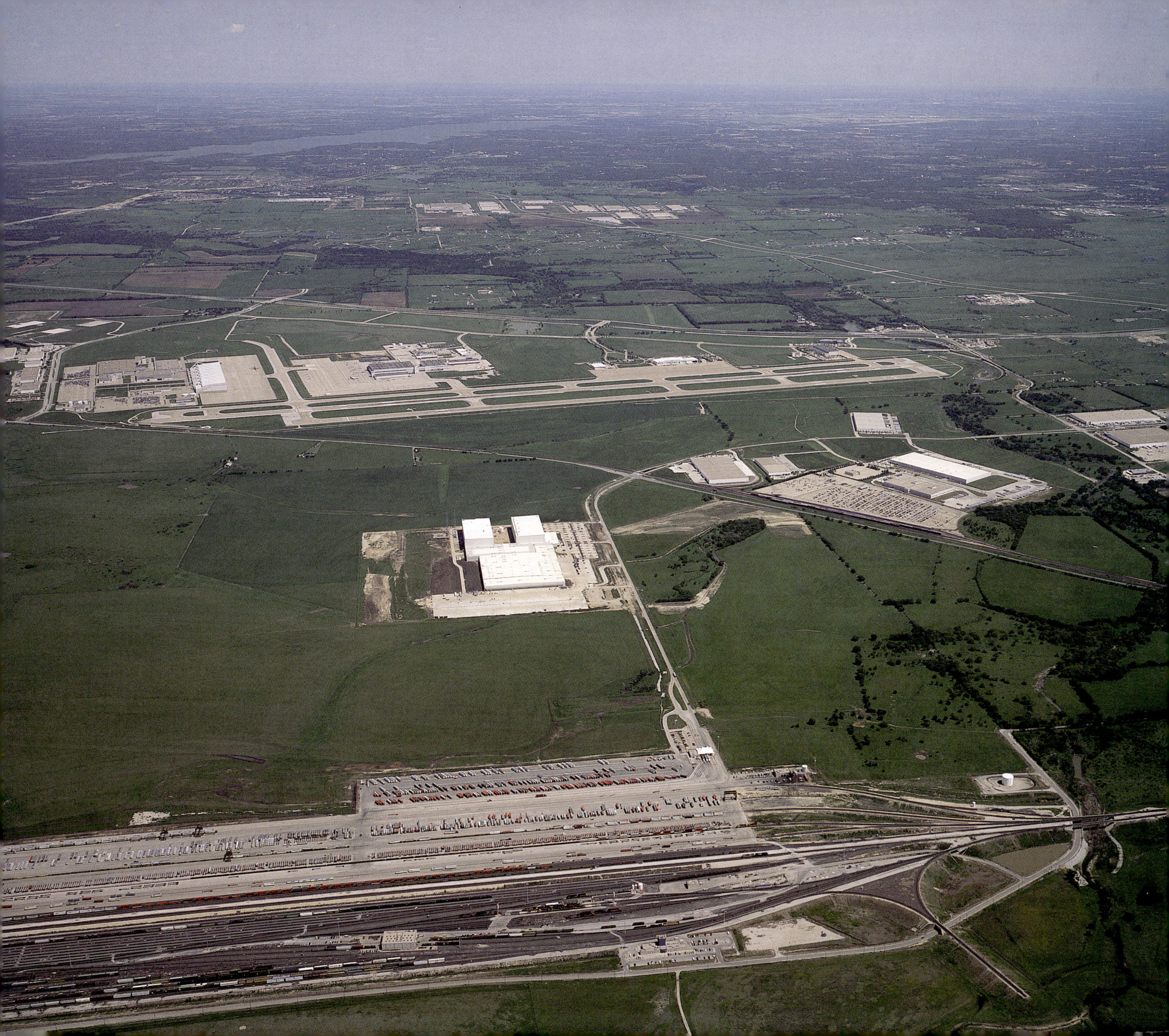

February 1991   *February 1993*   *April 1997*

Alliance Center

This 2,400-acre sector surrounding Fort Worth Alliance Airport offers sites for direct taxiway access. In fact, the majority of residents in Alliance Center are aviation-related companies, including Federal Express, American Airlines, Galaxy Aerospace, HeliFlite Shares, Bell Agusta Aerospace Corporation, Bell Helicopter Textron, the U.S. Drug Enforcement Administration, the Federal Aviation Administration, a U.S. Customs Office, ATC Group, DDH Aviation and Jet City. Service-related residents include the Alliance Opportunity Center, the Fort Worth Fire Department and Fort Worth Aviation Heritage Association, which oversees the annual Alliance airshow. At the airport, a fixed base operation managed by Alliance Aviation Services, has opened to accommodate corporate and general aviation aircraft and personnel.

Heritage Commons 1, the first speculative office building at Alliance, is located where Interstate 35W and Westport Parkway cross. The three-phase garden office complex consists of two-story buildings situated around a central commons area. Residents include Hillwood and the TCUglobalcenter, Texas Christian University's new facility that offers specialized education programs for the residents of Alliance and the surrounding communities. Other plans for Alliance Center include the Alliance World Trade Center, a facility that will house firms involved in global commerce.

April 1999

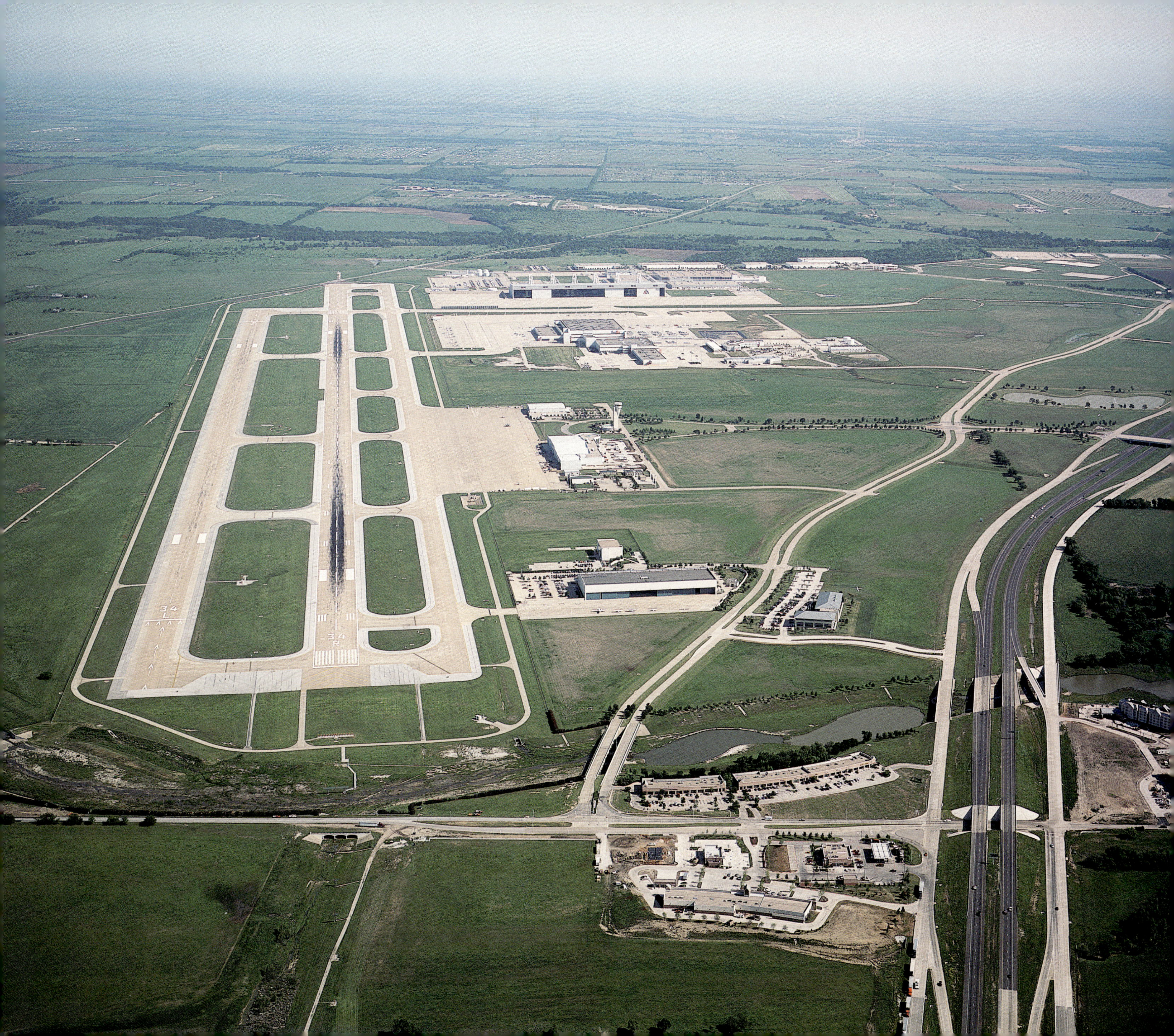
34 L
34 R

February 1993　　　*April 1995*　　　*May 1996*

Alliance Commerce Center

The Alliance Commerce Center is a 250-acre business park for small and medium-sized operations, located directly north of Fort Worth Alliance Airport.

Geared toward office, distribution, light manufacturing, high-tech, research-and-development and aviation-support firms, the area offers sites for purchase or lease. Residents include Patterson Dental, Nolato, Recaro Aircraft Seating, CompuCom Systems, Unison Industries, Rite Aid/PCS Health Systems, Savcor Coatings, Triple S Plastics and Alliance Operating Services.

April 1999

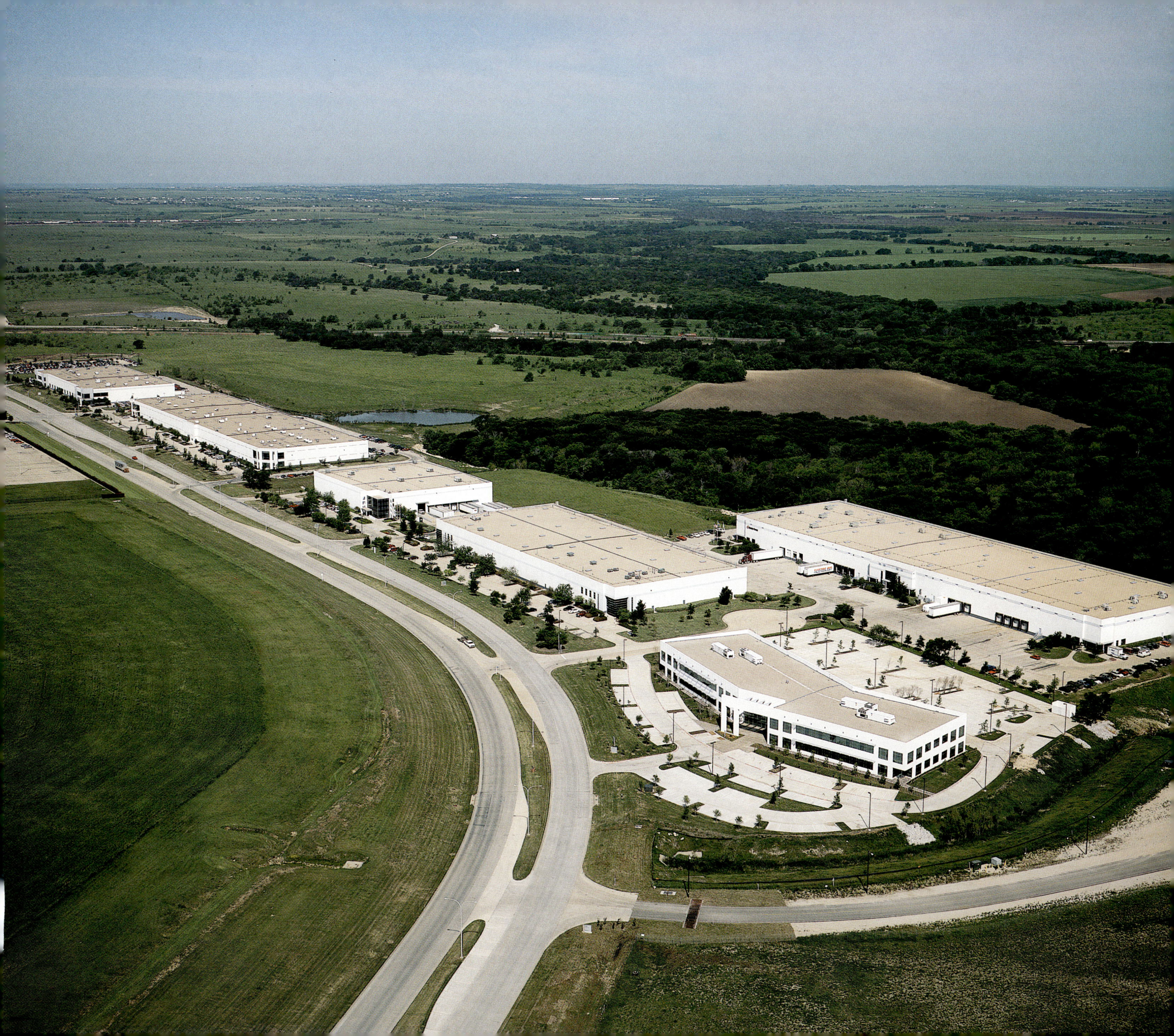

October 1991 *September 1994* *June 1997*

Alliance Crossing

Located on the southern edge of Alliance at Interstate 35W and Westport Parkway, Alliance Crossing is 250,000 square-feet of development designed to provide business and retail conveniences for Alliance-area employees and residents. Residents of Alliance Crossing include Cactus Flower Café, MedAlliance, Subway, TransTrade, Westaff, Mobil, Dr. Rajeev Misra, Fort Worth Police Department, Kinder Temporary Services, Westport Physical Therapy and Rehabilitation, Wendy's, Dallas Business Journal, Bank One, Sonny Bryan's Smokehouse, Hampton Inn, Hawthorn Suites, Norwest Bank, HighTech FotoSign, Pro-Cuts, Manpower, Schlotzsky's, Oriental Garden, Remedy Staffing, Taco Bueno and the U.S. Post Office.

April 1999

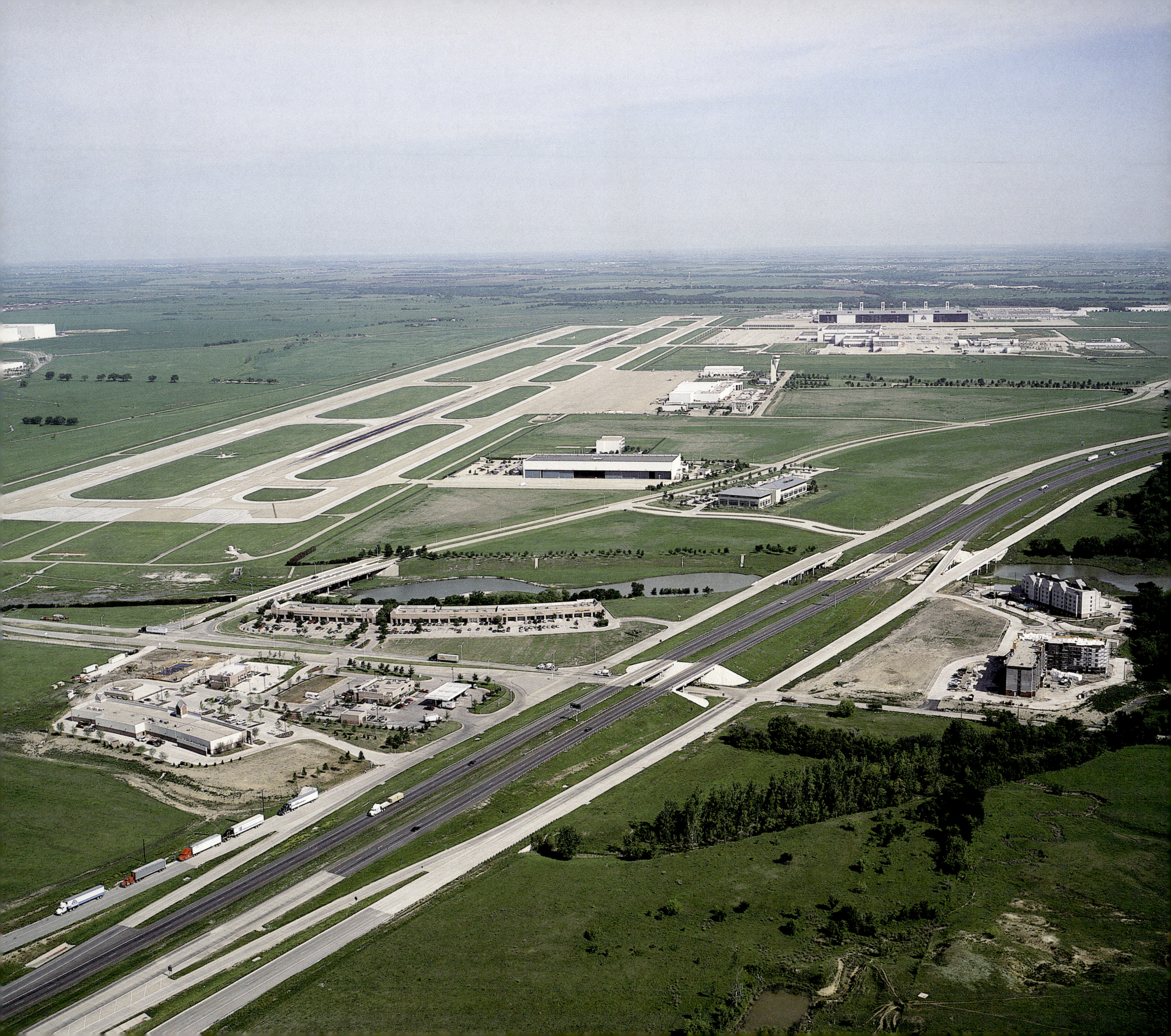

(left to right) Michael Spence of Valeo Electronics, Ross Perot Jr, Fort Worth Councilwoman Becky Haskin and Martin Haub of Valeo Electronics at the Valeo Electronics groundbreaking.

Alliance Advanced Technology Center

Located northeast of Fort Worth Alliance Airport and bisected by Interstate 35W, the 1,600-acre Alliance Advanced Technology Center is designed to create a new advanced-technology corridor in the region. This growing sector will be able to provide the type of business and physical environments needed by today's cutting-edge technology corporations. Moreover, it will expand upon the sophisticated infrastructure in place at Alliance.

The Alliance Advanced Technology Center is the site of Intel's planned $1.3 billion advanced logic wafer fabrication plant, set on 532 acres. The 745 acres adjacent to the site is targeted for the numerous technology-related companies expected to locate near the microprocessor chip maker's facility. In September of 1999, Valeo Electronics purchased 7 acres to build a 65,000-square-foot electronics manufacturing facility.

Illustration of the Alliance Advanced Technology Center with the Intel property highlighted in blue and possible future construction rendered graphically

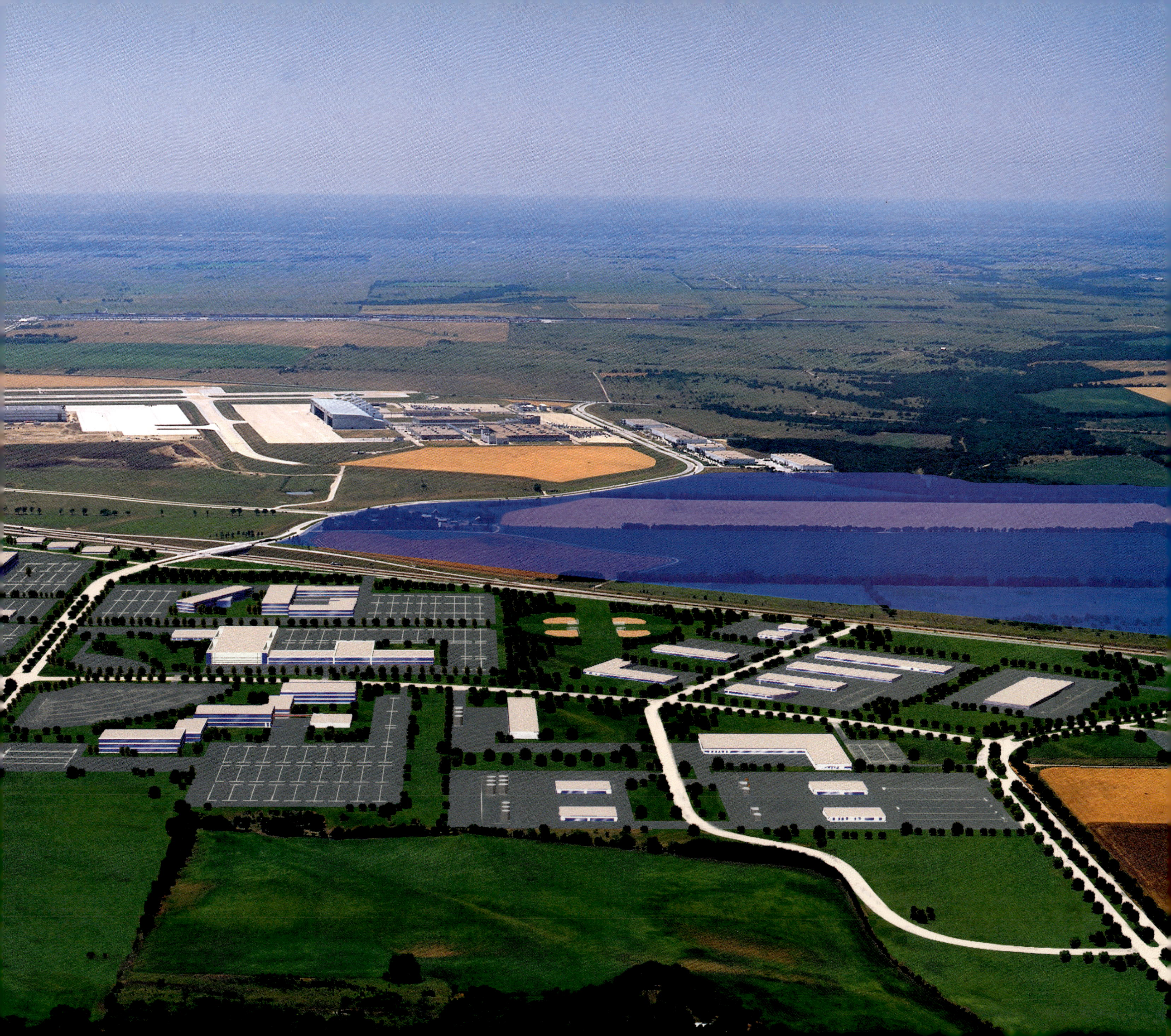

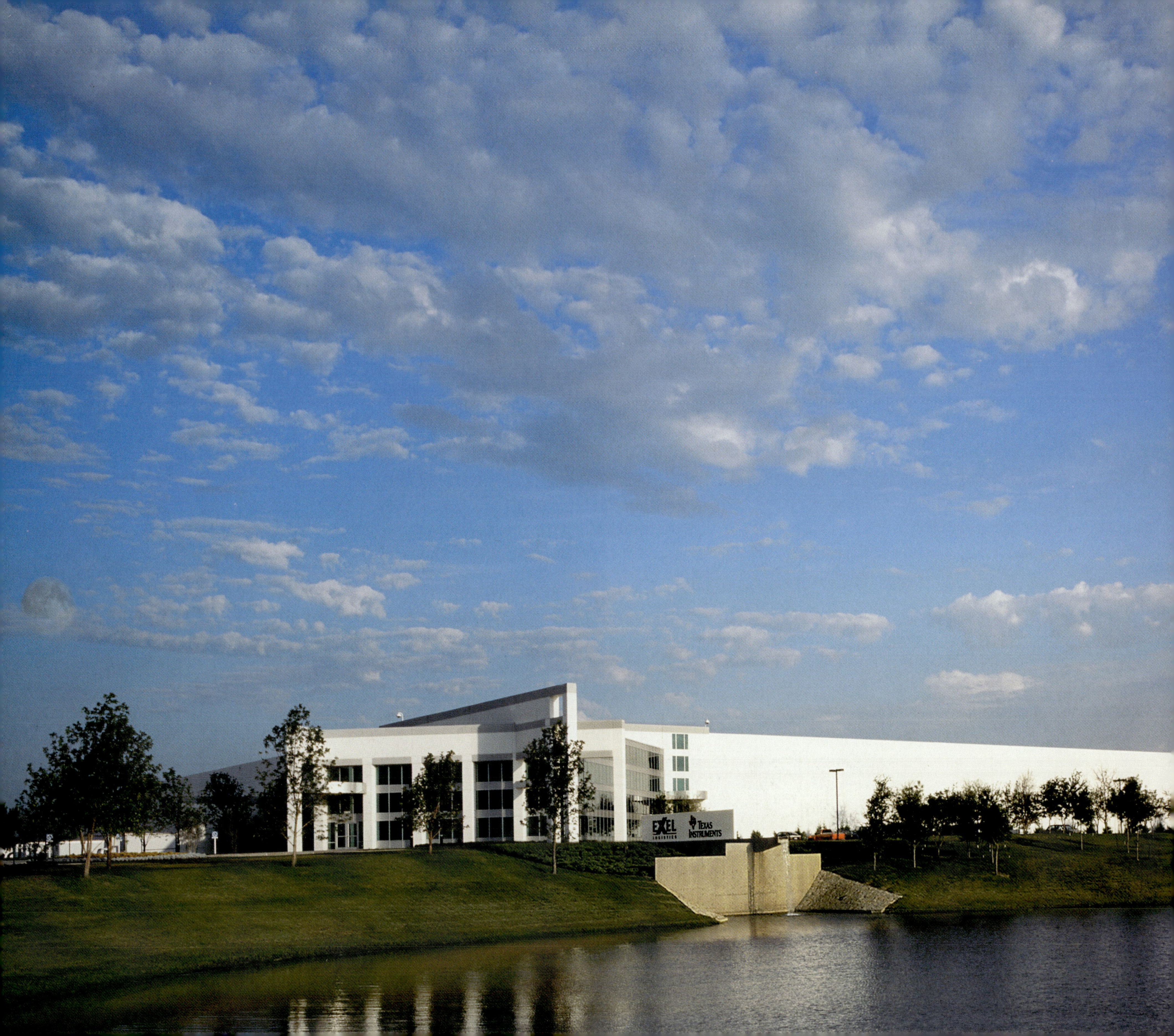
EXEL
Texas Instruments

Corporate Residents

Alliance Air Services and Alliance Aviation Services

American Airlines

Applied Industrial Technology

AT&T

Burlington Northern Santa Fe

Alliance Air Services
Alliance Aviation Services
Sector: Alliance Center
Sq. Ft.: 39,318
Employees: 27
AAiS Opening: January 1994
AAvS Opening: February 1994

Alliance Air Services, Hillwood's aviation management and service company, manages Alliance Airport for the city of Fort Worth. Alliance Aviation Services operates Hillwood's full-service fixed base operation at Fort Worth Alliance Airport.

Alliance Operating Services
Sector: Alliance Commerce Center
Sq. Ft.: 40,536
Employees: 5
JV formation: October 1998

A joint venture between Hillwood and Longistics, Alliance Operating Services provides third-party logistics services, such as utilizing the Alliance foreign trade zone.

Alliance Opportunity Center
Sector: Alliance Center
Sq. Ft.: 3,466
Employees: 7
Opening: May 1998

Established by Tarrant County College, Tarrant County Workforce Board, North Center Texas Workforce Board and Hillwood, the Alliance Opportunity Center finds and trains employees for Alliance businesses.

American Airlines
Sector: Alliance Center
Sq. Ft.: 1,600,000
Employees: 2,000
Announcement: June 1989

American Airlines, a Fortune 500 company, operates a $481 million aircraft maintenance and engineering center from its complex, which houses the largest single cantilever building in the world.

Ameritrade
Sector: Alliance Gateway
Sq. Ft.: 187,644
Employees: 1,000
Announcement: March 1999

Ameritrade, an online brokerage firm, operates a call center & customer service center.

Applied Industrial Technologies
Sector: Alliance Gateway
Sq. Ft.: 127,000
Employees: 80
Announcement: September 1996

Applied Industrial Technologies operates a manufacturing and distribution facility at Alliance. The company produces specialty bearings, transmission components and other industrial parts.

ATC Group
Sector: Alliance Center
Sq. Ft.: 4,298
Employees: 4
Lease signed: October 1997

The ATC Group provides aviation simulator flight training in the Fort Worth Alliance Airport hangar.

AT&T
Sector: Alliance Gateway
Sq. Ft.: 221,331
Employees: 100
Lease signed: 1994

AT&T, a Fortune 500 company, maintains a cellular phone fulfillment center at Alliance. Logistics Services coordinates the national distribution of AT&T's wireless service products.

Bank One Texas
Sector: Alliance Crossing
Sq. Ft.: 54
Employees: 0
Lease signed: June 1996

Bank One Texas offers an Automated Teller Machine within the convenience center at Alliance Crossing.

Bell Helicopter Textron
Sector: Alliance Center
Sq. Ft.: 367
Employees: 3
Lease signed: April 1997

Bell Helicopter Textron maintains an office at Fort Worth Alliance Airport where it is involved in helicopter sales and training.

Bell/Agusta Aerospace Company
Sector: Alliance Center
Sq. Ft.: 29,225
Employees: 50 with a potential for 200
Announcement: July 1999

Bell/Agusta Aerospace Company, a joint venture between Fort Worth-based Bell Helicopter Textron and Italian firm Agusta, is developing its new 15-acre headquarters at Alliance for its civilian tilt-rotor operations. At Alliance, the company will develop, manufacture and market its BA 609, the world's first civilian certificated tilt-rotor, as well as the AB 139, a medium twin-engine helicopter. The headquarters also will serve as a training site for pilots and mechanics and a delivery center. Training programs will begin in 2001 with the first BA 609 deliveries scheduled for 2002.

Beverage Canners International
Sector: Alliance Gateway
Sq. Ft.: 183,423
Employees: 65
Lease signed: March 1998

Beverage Canners International Corporation (BCI) is the largest independent soda, juice and water bottler in the country. Their Alliance operation features a new state-of-the-art bottling and distribution facility and distributes Samantha Springs drinking, spring and distilled water among its product lines. Samantha Springs, a natural spring in Keller, Texas, is named after the owner's daughter who died of a heart defect. A portion of the proceeds from the Samantha Springs, label is dedicated to funding heart defect research and promoting organ donation.

Burlington Northern Santa Fe

Sector: Westport at Alliance
Sq. Ft.: 108,000
Employees: 295
Announcement: May 1989

Burlington Northern Santa Fe, a Fortune 500 firm, operates two facilities at Alliance: the BNSF Automotive Facility and the BNSF Intermodal Hub Center. Handling over 100,000 vehicles annually, the 55-acre Auto Facility serves as a distribution port for Daimler Chrysler, American Honda, Hyundai and Kia. The 735-acre, $115 million intermodal yard is one of the largest intermodal facilities in the country.

Cactus Flower Cafe

Sector: Alliance Crossing
Sq. Ft.: 5,546
Employees: 34
Opening: October 1992

With four locations, Cactus Flower Cafe is a Fort Worth-owned family-dining restaurant.

Children's Courtyard

Sector: Alliance Gateway
Sq. Ft.: 13,600
Employees: 20
Announcement: June 1999

Children's Courtyard is the first child-care center at Alliance. The center will provide a wide range of services for approximately 190 infants, toddlers and pre school children.

CompuCom Systems

Sector: Alliance Commerce Center
Sq. Ft.: 96,283
Employees: 85
Opening: January 1995

A national distributor and integrator of personal computers and software, CompuCom Systems operates a national distribution center at Alliance.

DDH Aviation

Sector: Alliance Center
Sq. Ft.: 670
Employees: 4
Lease signed: February 1998

DDH Aviation serves as an aircraft broker, buying and selling airplanes, within the FBO at Fort Worth Alliance Airport.

DSC Logistics

Sector: Alliance Gateway
Sq. Ft.: 600,000
Employees: 250
Announcement: October 1998

DSC Logistics is the first resident in the recent 850-acre expansion of Alliance Gateway. The company is the nation's largest privately owned third-party logistics provider.

Dallas Business Journal

Sector: Alliance Crossing
Sq. Ft.: 974
Employees: 4
Lease signed: December 1998

Owned by parent company American City Business Journals, The Dallas Business Journal operates a Tarrant/Denton County bureau at Alliance Crossing.

Federal Aviation Administration

Sector: Alliance Center
Control Tower Sq. Ft.: 40,000
Office Sq. Ft.: 7,706
Employees: 43
At Alliance since: December 1989

The FAA operates the Fort Worth Alliance Airport Air Traffic Control Tower, a Flight Standards District Office and an Airways Facilities Sector field office in Alliance Center, supervising aircraft, agencies and personnel in 30 Texas counties.

Federal Express

Sector: Alliance Center
Sq. Ft.: 986,000
Employees: 975
Announcement: December 1993

Federal Express, a Fortune 500 firm, is the world's largest express transportation company. The Southwest Regional Hub at Alliance is the company's only completely automated hub and includes seven buildings, aircraft ramp areas and parking for delivery trucks. In August 1999, a day shift was added to the sorting hub, increasing the number of packages handled daily and nightly to 175,000.

Fort James

Sector: Alliance Gateway
Sq. Ft.: 375,000
Employees: 85
Announcement: March 1996

Fort James, formerly James River Paper, is a Fortune 500 manufacturer of paper products. The company operates a regional distribution center at Alliance.

Fort Worth Aviation Heritage Association

Sector: Alliance Center
Sq. Ft.: 1,890
Employees: 2
At Alliance since: 1994

The Fort Worth Aviation Heritage Association operates a 1,890-square-foot office in Alliance Center. The association coordinates the annual International Air Show at Fort Worth Alliance Airport.

Fort Worth Fire Department

Sector: Alliance Center
Sq. Ft.: 2,000
Employees: 43
At Alliance since: 1989

The city of Fort Worth Fire Department operates a fire station at Alliance Center.

Fort Worth Police Department

Sector: Alliance Crossing
Sq. Ft.: 730
Employees: 3
Lease signed: April 1998

The city of Fort Worth Police Department operates a police substation from the retail center.

Galaxy Aerospace

Sector: Alliance Center
Sq. Ft.: 160,897
Employees: 185
Announcement: August 1997

One of business aviation's most dynamic companies, Galaxy Aerospace recently moved into a state-of-the-art hangar and headquarters at Alliance. The Astra SPX and Galaxy corporate jets are completed and serviced at the Alliance facility.

Galaxy Aerospace

Fort Worth Fire Departmant

Fort James

Federal Express

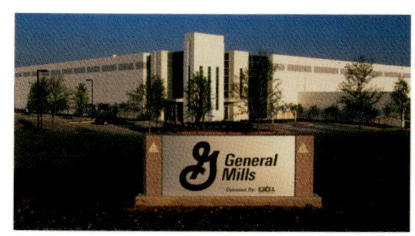

General Mills
Sector: Westport at Alliance
Sq. Ft.: 367,815
Employees: 100
Lease signed: June 1997

General Mills, an international food company, maintains a distribution center at Alliance. The center is operated by Exel Logistics North America, a worldwide provider of warehousing and distribution services.

Hampton Inn & Suites
Sector: Alliance Crossing
Sq. Ft.: 90,000
Employees: 25
Announcement: April 1997

A 95-room facility, the Hampton Inn & Suites serves as the first hotel at Alliance. The property is designed with traditional guest rooms for short stays and suites for long-term accommodations.

Hawthorn Suites
Sector: Alliance Crossing
Sq. Ft.: 91,476
Employees: 20
Announcement: December 1997

A 120-room extended-stay hotel, Hawthorn Suites is the second hotel at Alliance.

HeliFlite Shares
Sector: Alliance Center
Sq. Ft.: 2,000
Employees: 10
At Alliance since: November 1998

HeliFlite Shares, an innovator in corporate helicopter fractional ownership, recently moved from an office in Alliance Crossing to a larger space in Alliance Center.

Hewlett-Packard/Ryder Integrated Logistics
Sector: Alliance Gateway
Sq. Ft.: 192,177
Employees: 20
Lease signed: August 1999

Hewlett-Packard, a Fortune 500 firm, operates a national distribution center at Alliance for the company's Pavilion line of home computer products. The facility is managed by Ryder Integrated Logistics, one of the world's leaders in logistics services.

HighTech FotoSign
Sector: Alliance Crossing
Sq. Ft.: 1,174
Employees: 2
Lease signed: April 1998

HighTech FotoSign designs, produces and manufactures signage from their location in the Alliance Crossing retail area.

Hillwood
Sector: Alliance Center
Sq. Ft.: 20,676
Employees: 79
At Alliance since: 1988

The developer of Alliance, Hillwood oversees its property development in Tarrant County and Denton County from its offices in Heritage Commons.

Intel
Sector: Alliance Advanced Technology Center
Estimated Sq. Ft.: 800,000
Employees: Potential for 1,000
Announcement: November 1996

Intel, a Fortune 500 firm, is the world's largest producer of microprocessors and a leading manufacturer of personal computer networking and communications products. Intel currently operates a 50,000-square-foot office at Alliance and plans to build a new chip fabrication complex, which will serve as the anchor for the Alliance Advanced Technology Center.

International Aviation Composites
Sector: Westport at Alliance
Sq. Ft.: 20,000
Employees: 20
Announcement: July 1997

International Aviation Composites purchased two acres for its corporate headquarters and aviation service facility. IAC provides a variety of helicopter repair and maintenance services for Aerospatiale, Bell Helicopter, MBB and McDonnell Douglas.

JCPenney
Sector: Westport at Alliance
Sq. Ft.: 1.2 million
Employees: 400
Announcement: October 1996

The new, state-of-the-art JCPenney Distribution Center at Alliance features one of the largest steel rack-supported systems in the nation. With 17 levels and 105 bays of storage space, the 145,520 load cells can store approximately 72,000 pounds of merchandise. Scheduled to open in mid-2000, the distribution center will utilize JCPenney's Automated Case Receiving System to annually process 10,000 to 13,000 shipping containers from international ports, taking advantage of its proximity to the intermodal yard at Alliance.

Jet City, Inc.
Sector: Alliance Center
Sq. Ft.: 502
Employees: N/A
Lease signed: April 1999

Jet City provides aircraft-related services, including maintenance, sales and charter services, from its location at Fort Worth Alliance Airport.

John Deere
Sector: Alliance Gateway
Sq. Ft.: 287,240
Employees: 20
Lease signed: March 1999

John Deere is the world's leading producer of agricultural equipment. The Fortune 500 company, which also produces industrial equipment, distributes gasoline-powered consumer lawn and garden equipment from its Alliance warehouse.

Kinder Temporary Services
Sector: Alliance Crossing
Sq. Ft.: 974
Employees: 3
Lease signed: May 1996

Kinder Temporary Services provides office, clerical and light manufacturing support on a temporary basis.

General Mills

Hampton Inn & Suites

HighTech FotoSign

JCPenney

Kraft Foods
Sector: Westport at Alliance
Sq. Ft.: 650,000
Employees: 220
Announcement: February 1997
Kraft Foods maintains a Southwest distribution campus, one of the largest facilities at Alliance.

MagneTek
Sector: Alliance Gateway
Sq. Ft.: 109,116
Employees: 35
Announcement: August 1997
MagneTek, a leading manufacturer of energy-saving electrical and electronic equipment, utilizes its 109,116-square-foot site for its national distribution center.

Manpower
Sector: Alliance Crossing
Sq. Ft.: 1,523
Employees: 4
Lease signed: October 1998
Manpower, a Fortune 500 firm, provides staffing, training and temporary employment services.

Marriott Distribution Services
Sector: Westport at Alliance
Sq. Ft.: 127,200
Employees: 70
Opening: December 1995
Marriott Distribution Services, a division of Fortune 500 Marriott International, operates a food-service distribution center.

Maytag
Sector: Westport at Alliance
Sq. Ft.: 237,000
Employees: 25
Opening: June 1996
The Fortune 500 firm and internationally known appliance manufacturer operates a regional distribution center at Alliance.

MedAlliance
Sector: Alliance Crossing
Sq. Ft.: 6,716
Employees: 15
Opening: October 1992
MedAlliance provides medical services from its diagnostic medical and occupational health center in the retail center.

Michaels Stores
Sector: Westport at Alliance
Sq. Ft.: 407,000
Employees: 200
Opening: May 1996
Michaels Stores, the world's largest retailer of arts, crafts, framing, floral, decorative wall decor and seasonal merchandise, utilizes its 430,000-square-foot Alliance warehouse for a regional distribution facility.

Dr. Rajeev Misra, D.D.S.
Sector: Alliance Crossing
Sq. Ft.: 1,218
Employees: 4
Lease signed: March 1996
Dr. Rajeev Misra provides dental services, specializing in general and cosmetic dentistry from his office in the retail center.

Mitsubishi Motor Sales of America
Sector: Alliance Gateway
Sq. Ft.: 203,000
Employees: 250
Announcement: July 1996
Mitsubishi Motor Sales of America, the domestic subsidiary of Japanese Mitsubishi Group, operates a regional parts distribution facility at Alliance.

Mobil
Sector: Alliance Crossing
Sq. Ft.: 2,579
Employees: 4
Opening: January 1996
Mobil, a Fortune 500 company, maintains a gasoline service station, convenience store and car wash at Alliance Crossing.

Nestlé
Sector: Alliance Gateway
Sq. Ft.: 520,000
Employees: 100
Announcement: May 1992
Nestlé, the world's largest food company, operates a $20 million distribution center at Alliance.

Nokia
Sector: Alliance Gateway
Sq. Ft.: 498,195
Employees: 2,830
Announcement: November 1994
Nokia is the world's leading mobile phone supplier. The company operates two facilities at Alliance: a cellular phone manufacturing plant and distribution center and a service and repair center. In December 1998, the Alliance facility manufactured Nokia's 100 millionth cellular phone.

Nolato
Sector: Alliance Commerce Center
Sq. Ft.: 39,884
Employees: 50
Announcement: December 1998
Nolato supplies high-precision injection plastic components to mobile phone manufacturers, including Alliance resident Nokia.

Norwest Bank
Sector: Alliance Crossing
Sq. Ft.: 3,706
Employees: 6
Lease signed: January 1999
Norwest Bank, a Fortune 500 firm that recently merged with Wells Fargo, serves as the first full-service bank at Alliance.

Oriental Garden
Sector: Alliance Crossing
Sq. Ft.: 4,145
Employees: 12
Lease signed: November 1998
Oriental Garden operates a Chinese buffet restaurant in the Alliance Crossing retail center.

Nestlé Warehouse

Mitsubishi

Michaels

Nokia

MagneTek

CORPORATE RESIDENTS · 1999

Schlotzsky's

Southwestern Bell

Perlos

Patterson Dental

PCS Health Systems

PC Service Source
Sector: Alliance Gateway
Sq. Ft.: 204,020
Employees: 85
Opening: December 1995
With its Alliance distribution center, PC Service Source serves as an efficient, cost-effective hub for national distribution of its computer parts.

PCS Health Systems
Sector: Alliance Commerce Center
Sq. Ft.: 93,764
Employees: 200
Announcement: March 1996
PCS Health Systems, a division of pharmaceutical company Rite Aid, operates a national mail-order pharmacy and fulfillment center at Alliance.

Patterson Dental
Sector: Alliance Commerce Center
Sq. Ft.: 52,850
Employees: 50
Announcement: May 1993
Patterson Dental, one of the nation's largest distributors of dental products, was the first customer in the Alliance Commerce Center.

Perlos
Sector: Alliance Gateway
Sq. Ft.: 181,039
Employees: 150
Opening: May 1995
A Finnish manufacturer of exterior parts for cellular telephones, Perlos, Inc. operates a manufacturing, distribution and assembly center at Alliance. Perlos, a supplier to Nokia, recently expanded their facility by 98,000 square feet.

Pro-Cuts
Sector: Alliance Crossing
Sq. Ft.: 879
Employees: 6
Lease signed: August 1998
Pro-Cuts is the largest hair-care franchise in Texas and the sixth largest in the nation. The company has an outlet in the retail center.

Randalls Food Markets
Sector: Alliance Gateway
Sq. Ft.: 976,471
Employees: 360
Lease signed: January 1999
The lease of 976,471 square feet to Randalls Food Markets for a distribution center marks the largest lease at Alliance. The company, which operates Randalls, Tom Thumb and Simon David grocery stores, distributes products to its North Texas stores from its Alliance facility.

Recaro Aircraft Seating
Sector: Alliance Commerce Center
Sq. Ft.: 61,088
Employees: 60
Announcement: April 1999
Germany-based Recaro Aircraft Seating leases space in Alliance Commerce Center for its first U.S. assembly hub. The location of its manufacturing facility allows the company to supply airline seats to one of its major customers, Alliance resident American Airlines.

Remedy Staffing
Sector: Alliance Crossing
Sq. Ft.: 2,800
Employees: 3
Lease signed: March 1999
Remedy Staffing, a personnel staffing agency, provides employment services from their location in the retail center.

Savcor Coatings
Sector: Alliance Commerce Center
Sq. Ft.: 42,025
Employees: 60-80
Announcement: October 1999
Savcor Coatings, the world's leading producer of PVD-coatings, applies metal coatings to plastic parts for such items as mobile phones, computers and pagers. Savcor Coatings is the newest addition at Alliance to the fast-growing supply chain for Nokia.

SC Johnson Wax
Sector: Westport at Alliance
Sq. Ft.: 192,000
Employees: 35
Announcement: April 1997
SC Johnson Wax is the leading manufacturer and distributor of consumer and commercial wax products. The company maintains a warehouse and distribution center at Alliance.

Schlotzsky's
Sector: Alliance Crossing
Sq. Ft.: 3,200
Employees: 20
Opening: March 1999
Schlotzsky's, best known for its deli-style sandwiches and sourdough bread, provides a unique line of freshly prepared food in a "fast-casual" atmosphere.

Sonny Bryan's Smokehouse
Sector: Alliance Crossing
Sq. Ft.: 4,334
Employees: 15
Lease signed: October 1996
Sonny Bryan's Smokehouse features a variety of smoked meat meals in its barbecue restaurant in the retail center.

Southwestern Bell Telephone
Sector: Alliance Gateway
Sq. Ft.: 215,062
Employees: 850
Announcement: May 1997
Southwestern Bell, which operates a call center and work center at Alliance, was the first large-scale office occupant for the Alliance development.

Subway Restaurant
Sector: Alliance Crossing
Sq. Ft.: 1,217
Employees: 14
Opening: May 1993
Subway Restaurant, the world's largest submarine sandwich franchise and second-largest food franchiser, operates a delicatessen and sandwich shop in the retail center.

Sunstate Equipment Company

Sector: Westport at Alliance
Sq. Ft.: 8,000
Employees: 20
Announcement: February 1998

Sunstate Equipment Company rents construction and industrial equipment from its branch office at Alliance.

Taco Bueno

Sector: Alliance Crossing
Sq. Ft.: 2,850
Employees: 10
Announcement: April 1999

Taco Bueno operates a quick-service restaurant offering menu items of freshly prepared traditional Mexican meals from its location in Alliance Crossing.

Tech Data

Sector: Alliance Gateway
Sq. Ft.: 539,000
Employees: 250
Announcement: March 1996

Fortune 500 firm Tech Data, a computer parts and software company, operates a national distribution center from its Alliance facility.

Texas Christian University

Sector: Alliance Center
Sq. Ft.: 15,784
Employees: 5
Announcement: September 1999

Texas Christian University operates the TCUglobalcenter at Alliance, an education center offering undergraduate and graduate programs to the corporate and residential communities within the Alliance corridor. The facility features a 72-person, state-of-the-art tiered classroom, two 30-person classrooms, two large conference rooms and flexible meeting/classroom spaces.

Texas Instruments

Sector: Alliance Gateway
Sq. Ft.: 409,914
Employees: 350
Announcement: August 1996

Texas Instruments, a Fortune 500 firm, is a global semiconductor company and the world's leading designer and supplier of digital signal processing and analog technologies. Exel Logistics, a provider of warehousing, distribution and value-added services, supports Texas Instruments computer chip distribution for North America at Alliance.

Trans-Trade

Sector: Alliance Crossing
Sq. Ft.: 727
Employees: 3
Lease signed: November 1994

Trans-Trade operates a freight forwarding service from its location at Alliance Crossing.

Triple S Plastics

Sector: Alliance Commerce Center
Sq. Ft.: 60,000
Employees: 80 with the potential for 140
Lease signed: June 1999

Triple S Plastics, a full-service custom injection molder, operates a manufacturing facility at Alliance specifically equipped for the telecommunications and high-technology industries. The company's arrival at Alliance allows a closer connection to one of its customers, Alliance resident Nokia.

Tucker Rocky Distributing

Sector: Alliance Gateway
Sq. Ft.: 177,632
Employees: 125
Announcement: August 1997

Tucker Rocky Distributing maintains its corporate headquarters and distribution center at Alliance for its motorcycle, snowmobile, watercraft and bicycle parts and accessories.

U.S. Customs Office

Sector: Alliance Center
Sq. Ft.: 106
Employees: 2
Opening: October 1993

Fort Worth Alliance Airport offers customs services through the U.S. Customs Office at the Fixed Base Operation.

U.S. Drug Enforcement Administration

Sector: Alliance Center
Sq. Ft.: 160,000
Employees: 215
Announcement: January 1991

The U.S. Drug Enforcement Administration operates its National Airwing Headquarters, which includes administrative support offices and maintenance facilities for its fleet of aircraft, at Alliance.

U.S. Post Office

Sector: Alliance Crossing
Sq. Ft.: 5,809
Employees: 5
Lease signed: March 1999

The U.S. Post Office operates a full-service retail outlet in Alliance Crossing.

Unison Industries

Sector: Alliance Commerce Center
Sq. Ft.: 58,433
Employees: 250
Opening: April 1996

Formerly BFGoodrich Aerospace, Unison Industries maintains its division headquarters at Alliance for the distribution of the Electrical Interconnect product line of its Engine Electrical Systems Division.

Valeo Electronics

Sector: Alliance Advanced Technology Center
Sq. Ft.: 65,000
Employees: 170
Announcement: September 1999

Valeo, a global leader in the supply of components, systems and modules to the automotive industry, will operate a highly automated electronics manufacturing facility at the Alliance Advanced Technology Center. The facility will be completed in the spring of 2000 with production beginning in late summer.

Tech Data

Texas Instruments

Tucker Rocker Distributing

U.S. Drug Enforcement Administration

Zenith Electronics

W.W. Grainger

W.W. Grainger
Sector: Westport at Alliance
Sq. Ft.: 160,153
Employees: 150
Lease signed: August 1998
The Fortune 500 company is the leading business-to-business distributor of maintenance, repair and operating supplies.

Wendy's
Sector: Alliance Crossing
Sq. Ft.: 2,331
Employees: 20
Opening: January 1996
Wendy's operates a quick-service restaurant in the convenience center.

Westaff
Sector: Alliance Crossing
Sq. Ft.: 1,002
Employees: 3
Opening: March 1995
Formerly Personnel Connections, Westaff offers temporary and full-time staffing services, with offices in Texas, Florida and California.

Westport Physical Therapy and Rehabilitation Center
Sector: Alliance Crossing
Sq. Ft.: 2,922
Employees: 5
Lease signed: June 1996
The center provides general orthopedic physical therapy, industrial rehabilitation, sports rehabilitation and aquatic therapy from its facility in the retail center.

Zenith Electronics
Sector: Alliance Gateway
Sq. Ft.: 499,797
Employees: 100
Announcement: August 1994
A leading manufacturer of consumer electronics and television products, Zenith Electronics operates a distribution facility at Alliance.